I0116888

WORLD EMPLOYMENT PROGRAMME

Background Papers for Training in
Population, Human Resources and Development Planning

Paper No. 6

ASSESSING WOMEN'S ECONOMIC CONTRIBUTIONS TO DEVELOPMENT

by

Ruth Dixon-Mueller and Richard Anker

Published with the financial support
of the United Nations Population Fund

INTERNATIONAL LABOUR OFFICE   GENEVA

Copyright © International Labour Organization 1988

Publications of the International Labour Office enjoy copyright under Protocol 2 of the Universal Copyright Convention. Nevertheless, short excerpts from them may be reproduced without authorization, on condition that the source is indicated. For rights of reproduction or translation, application should be made to the Publications Branch (Rights and Permissions), International Labour Office, CH-1211 Geneva 22, Switzerland. The International Labour Office welcomes such applications.

ISBN 92-2-106796-3
ISSN 0258-2406

First published 1988
Third impression 1993

The designations employed in ILO publications, which are in conformity with United Nations practice, and the presentation of material therein do not imply the expression of any opinion whatsoever on the part of the International Labour Office concerning the legal status of any country, area or territory or of its authorities, or concerning the delimitation of its frontiers. The responsibility for opinions expressed in signed articles, studies and other contributions rests solely with their authors, and publication does not constitute an endorsement by the International Labour Office of the opinions expressed in them. Reference to names of firms and commercial products and processes does not imply their endorsement by the International Labour Office, and any failure to mention a particular firm, commercial product or process is not a sign of disapproval.

ILO publications can be obtained through major booksellers or ILO local offices in many countries, or direct from ILO Publications, International Labour Office, CH-1211 Geneva 22, Switzerland. A catalogue or list of new publications will be sent free of charge from the above address.

Printed by the International Labour Office, Geneva, Switzerland

PREFACE

This is the sixth in the series of background papers prepared as part of the ongoing ILO training activities in the area of population, human resources and development planning. For a description of the major training activities and of the programme under which these are conducted see <u>Population, human resources and development planning: the ILO contribution</u> (Geneva, ILO, 1987). The main objective of the programme is to help member States incorporate demographic elements into employment-related policies and, more broadly, to facilitate the integration of population and human resources development issues into national development planning.

The present paper addresses the issue of assessing women's contribution to economic development. This, as was emphasised in numerous national and international conferences held to mark the United Nations Decade for Women, 1975-85, is a subject area of great topical importance to development planners, policy makers, statisticians and researchers alike. Previous research and technical co-operation work by the ILO and other international bodies have highlighted the precarious socio-economic position of women. The need for improving women's roles in the economic development effort has been widely recognised by governments as a national economic and social goal. However, in general neither have the constraints been fully identified nor have specific policies and action programmes been adequately developed for achieving this goal.

It would be useful to draw the attention of the reader to the work which has been carried out at the ILO over the last few years under a large policy research programme in the field of women, population and development. A series of country studies has been undertaken which has included reviews of data collection techniques and identification of reasons for the underreporting of women's labour force activity in the official national statistics of many developing countries. A second set of studies focussed on government policies and measures aimed at improving the position of women and, more generally, at promoting development and its positive effects on women. These pointed out the significance of policy relevant issues, such as the adverse effects on socio-economic planning of inadequate documentation of women's productive activities, the failure to take account of the complexity of their familial roles, the profound effects on policy formulation of stereotyped models of sex roles, etc. A third set of studies involved investigation of sex inequalities and sex segregation of occupations and labour markets. In indicating that women's role in reproduction and the resulting costs perceived by the employer are among the major reasons why employers are reluctant to hire women, this investigation underscores the need for policies that will reduce this disadvantage if women are ever to achieve equality of opportunity and break out of the vicious circle of high fertility and economic marginalisation. For a description of major studies released recently see Population and labour research news, 10 (Geneva, ILO, 1987).

Drawing upon the results of the above policy research work, the present paper makes a convincing argument that the absence of accurate information and analysis of women's productive activities in different economic sectors inevitably results in the under-utilisation or mis-use of female human resources. It assesses the extent of undercounting of economically active women, and identifies the major definitional and data collection problems which contribute to this. Additional dimensions of women's economic contribution from the perspective of time use and returns to labour are highlighted. The paper presents several approaches to the assessment of women's economic contribution to development, and thereby emphasises the need for incorporating the analysis of women's roles and prevailing constraints on women's economic productivity into comprehensive population, human resources and development planning.

It is planned to prepare a sequel to this paper which would deal specifically with the issue of macro-level policy interventions, development planning approaches and action programmes for improving the roles and status of women as an integral part of a concerted national effort to social and economic development. In doing so, the paper would attempt to bring out the limitations of a strategy consisting primarily of women-specific projects and welfare programmes.

We would like to acknowledge with thanks the financial support of the United Nations Population Fund (UNFPA) for the population, human resources and development planning programme under which this series of training papers is being prepared.

Ghazi M. Farooq

CONTENTS

I. INTRODUCTION: WOMEN AND DEVELOPMENT PLANNING

The principle of integrating women into all phases of the development process -- both as participants in planning and policy-making and as beneficiaries -- has now become widely accepted by governments throughout the world. The importance of women's contributions to the achievement of national economic and social goals was initially articulated at the United Nations International Women's Year Conference in Mexico City in 1975. It has been stressed repeatedly in national and international conferences throughout the United Nations Decade for Women from 1975 to 1985. Participants at the end-of-decade conference held in Nairobi in 1985 emphasised once again that the neglect of women in development planning has had many deleterious effects, such as aggravating declines in food production in some areas and marginalising many women workers through the loss of income earning opportunities and their concentration in low income occupations. As a consequence, both rural and urban households have often faced increasing impoverishment and difficulty in meeting their basic needs. Women in this view are rightfully seen as actively integrated into economic life and their labour and economic output as essential for supporting their families.

One reason for the negative impact on women of development efforts aimed at maximising economic growth has been the tendency for national planning and resources to be concentrated in the industrialised and monetised sectors of the economy -- spheres that are mostly dominated by men (International Research and Training Institute for the Advancement of Women [INSTRAW], 1985). Informal sector activities and subsistence production on which family welfare is often heavily dependent and in which women's contributions are generally most significant have not been given the high priority they deserve. Yet even in agrarian reform programmes that were specifically intended to raise agricultural productivity, increase rural incomes and reduce inequities in access to land and other productive resources, women have often lost out in comparison with men in the distribution of land rights and other benefits (Palmer, 1985a).

The considerable interest in women and development generated in recent years has given rise to a multitude of well-intentioned women-specific projects and welfare programmes -- both governmental and nongovernmental -- at local and national levels. Their purpose has been to help redress on a small scale some of the inequities and neglect suffered by women in the process of social and economic change. Typically, such projects have provided health-related, educational, or social services or short-term skill development for income generation.

As a strategy, the women-specific programmes have played an important role in many settings. This is especially true where women's social and economic subordination is most extreme. Yet in the long run, this approach has not led to large-scale integration of women into economic development nor has it addressed the multi-faceted problems of women in developing nations. Women-specific programmes and projects -- responding as they do to immediate and urgent needs -- often lack adequate planning or co-ordination with national development priorities. The strategy of "remedial action" has also tended to isolate women's issues and women's programmes in the peripheries of development planning far from where the major decisions are made. Most important, it has segregated them from crucial economic and political resources directed at comprehensive development endeavours (Buvinic, 1983:24-29).

Effective utilisation of a country's human resources requires that all social groups share equally in the development effort and in the distribution of benefits. The exclusion of any one group from equal participation -- especially one representing half the population -- represents a drastic loss of human potential. Governments and international agencies now recognise that integrating women effectively and fully in the development process is not just a question of equity, but one of necessity for national and international progress.

But how is such integration to be accomplished? Planners face a number of difficulties in formulating policies and programmes to achieve this goal. Among them is the need to overcome deeply ingrained prejudices and assumptions about women's roles, such as the belief that programmes of benefit to men will automatically benefit women through shared household resources, or that promoting the integration of women into employment generating schemes cannot be justified where there is significant male under- or unemployment. Assumptions such as these obscure the critical importance of women's economic needs and contributions, especially in low income households.

Related to these assumptions, and of special concern in this paper, is the lack of good statistical information and research on women's productive activities in different spheres of the economy (which is not such a major problem for men); on the differential access of males and females at all ages to economic and social resources within the household, the community, and the nation; and on the institutional obstacles that prevent women from becoming full partners with men in the development effort. The absence of information and analysis inevitably results in the under-utilisation or mis-use of female human resources. It is in this respect that the importance of research on women and the collection of relevant data become necessary tools for successful development planning (INSTRAW, 1985). Once they are identified, severe inequities in the distribution of educational and employment opportunities and of production assets based on gender (and on class, caste, and ethnicity) can be corrected in order to release the productive potential of all members of society.

Responding to numerous recommendations of international conferences during the UN Decade for Women, the United Nations and its specialised agencies have embarked on a systematic effort to recommend and compile statistical indicators on women's condition for countries throughout the world (e.g., UN Statistical Office and INSTRAW, 1984; ILO and INSTRAW, 1985; INSTRAW and UN Statistical Office, 1986). The indicators are broad-ranging in their scope, including measures of family formation and dissolution, child-bearing, and household composition; formal schooling and vocational training; labour force participation; time use and household work; health and nutrition; mortality; national and international migration; and participation in political and cultural life. The purpose of this effort is to encourage governments and non-governmental organisations to <u>collect</u> relevant information systematically by gender (and age, class, ethnicity, and other relevant characteristics); to <u>analyse</u> such information in order to monitor progress and identify problem areas; and to <u>incorporate</u> findings on gender differences into planning and policy-making at the local and national levels.

The most common indicators of economic production, such as labour force statistics and systems of national accounts, have been heavily criticised for their tendency to underreport and undervalue women's work (e.g., Benería, 1982; Dixon, 1982; Anker, 1983). Not only are women often missed in the census counts of economically active populations, but the monetary value of their subsistence production to the household economy and thus to the national economy is often excluded from national accounts statistics. The use of biased economic indicators can lead to distorted perceptions of the nature of the economy and of a country's human resources. If women workers are selectively and extensively underenumerated, for example, as is the case in many developing countries, then aggregate labour force data used for planning purposes are useless. Errors in reporting the current size and occupational distribution of the labour force will be compounded by erroneous assumptions regarding trends and projections for the future.

The purpose of this paper is to present several approaches to the assessment of women's economic contributions to development. The discussion will focus on methods of measurement, on suggestions for data analysis, and on the relevance of findings to national planning. The portrayal of female labour force participation in official statistics is addressed in Section II. The following section identifies problems of definition and data collection that have led to the undercounting of economically active women in many countries. It also proposes some possible solutions. Section IV addresses several additional dimensions of economic activity from the perspective of women's contributions, such as time use and returns to labour. Suggestions for sample surveys that could compare the results of collecting labour force data in different ways are included in an Appendix. The intention of this entire review is to demonstrate the importance <u>and</u> usefulness of incorporating an analysis of women's economic roles --and analysis of prevailing constraints on their economic productivity -- into all aspects of population, human resources and development planning.

II. WOMEN IN THE LABOUR FORCE: STATISTICAL PROFILES

The most visible indicator of women's contribution to development is their labour force participation. The major official sources of information on the size and age-sex composition of the labour force are population censuses and national sample surveys. Censuses, generally taken every five or ten years, have the advantage of complete population coverage but the disadvantage of being cumbersome, expensive, and limited in the scope of the labour force information collected. Labour force or household surveys based on national samples can be taken more frequently (often annually) and can be tailored to specific informational requirements. Despite their smaller sample size, data from sample surveys can be representative of the country and are generally more reliable because interviewers are trained and supervised more carefully and questionnaires are more detailed.

Population censuses or surveys that include classifications of the economically active population by age, sex, occupation, and industry are available for only two-thirds of developing countries, however, and only one-third of those in sub-Saharan Africa (Table 1). Other countries have information for only one or two points in time. Thus there are large gaps in our knowledge of how the characteristics of the labour force differ from country to country and how they change over time. There are also serious problems with the comparability of existing data, especially with the enumeration of women who are unpaid family workers. This issue is discussed in section III below.

In an effort to fill some of these gaps, the International Labour Office (ILO) has prepared a set of labour force estimates and projections for all countries and world regions, including over 100 developing nations (ILO, 1977, 1986). The most recent publication includes estimates of the size and occupational structure of the labour force in each country, as well as activity rates by age and sex, for the years 1950, 1960, 1970, and 1980. Labour force projections are also estimated to the year 2025.

Like the population censuses, however, the ILO estimates for some countries are also of doubtful reliability where they depend on inadequate data for a particular country or on comparisons with neighbouring countries for their assumptions. Yet, despite their anomalies and shortcomings, by filling the gaps and bringing existing national labour force statistics into conformity with standard concepts of economic activity, they provide the best available data on

5

Table 1. Number and per centage of developing countries reporting national labour force data by age, sex, occupation, and industry, by region[a]

Region	Labour force by age and sex (%) (1)	Industrial classification (ISIC) by sex (%) (2)	Occupational classification (ISCO) by sex (%) (3)
Africa (Sub-Sahara) (N=36)	22 (61%)	12 (33%)	11 (31%)
North Africa and Middle East (N=17)	10 (59%)	13 (76%)	12 (71%)
Asia[b] (N=21)	15 (71%)	15 (71%)	15 (71%)
Latin America (N=23)	22 (96%)	20 (87%)	18 (78%)
Totals (N=97)	69 (71%)	60 (62%)	56 (58%)

Notes:

ISIC: International Standard Industrial Classification

ISCO: International Standard Classification of Occupations

a   Includes all developing countries with one million or more population in 1985 with relevant labour force data (since 1970) reported in source.

b   Includes Fiji.

Source: ILO, **Year Book of Labour Statistics**, various years (Geneva, ILO).

contrasting patterns of labour force participation among countries and world regions, and on past and future trends.

The remainder of this section reviews evidence from population censuses and surveys and from ILO estimates on several aspects of female labour force participation. It proceeds from a discussion of variations in economic activity rates by age and sex to the distribution of male and female workers according to occupation and employment status. The following section includes a critique of current labour force measures and provides some suggestions for their improvement. The purpose is to evaluate critically the current data sources and to propose ways in which accurate information on female labour force participation and associated characteristics can be useful to planners.

A. Economic Activity Rates by Sex and Age

As noted in the first paper in this training paper series for planners, the <u>economically active population</u> conventionally refers to the "total number of persons available for the production of economic goods and services, corresponding to the concept of income in national income statistics ..." (Farooq, 1985). It includes employed and unemployed persons and those seeking work for the first time. Activity <u>rates</u> refer to the number of economically active persons for every 100 persons in the base population, that is, to the <u>per centage</u> of the total population that is defined as economically active.

Economic activity rates are available for many countries in the **Year Book of Labour Statistics** published annually by the ILO. What do they tell us about the differences between men and women in their typical labour force profiles over the life cycle? Let us begin with an example from sub-Saharan Africa and then examine regional variations.

1. <u>Activity profiles: an African illustration</u>

Table 2 illustrates the standard format of published data on activity rates, based here on the 1982 population census of Zimbabwe. Column 10 presents additional calculations made for this paper. The table contains several types of information relevant to planners. First, although almost two-thirds of the total population aged 15 or above is economically active (column 3), there are important contrasts between the male population (80 per cent, column 6) and the female population (48 per cent, column 9). Second, the activity rates of males and females aged 15 to 19 are almost identical. But whereas the age-specific rates for men rise quickly to over 90 per cent for the prime working years, as is typical for most countries, those for women remain at about 50 per cent throughout their working, child-bearing, and child-rearing years. Third, the

Table 2. Total and economically active population by sex and age group, Zimbabwe population census, 1982
(numbers in thousands)

Age	Total			Males			Females			Female share of active pop.b (10)
	Total pop. (1)	Active pop. (2)	Activity ratea (3)	Total pop. (4)	Active pop. (5)	Activity ratea (6)	Total pop. (7)	Active pop. (8)	Activity ratea (9)	
0-14c	3,589	—	—	1,786	—	—	1,803	—	—	—
15-19	803	381	47.5	390	188	48.2	413	193	46.8	50.7
20-24	655	428	65.3	290	242	83.4	364	186	50.9	43.4
25-29	524	363	69.2	243	227	93.1	281	136	48.5	37.6
30-34	392	278	70.9	185	174	94.0	207	104	50.2	37.4
35-39	318	227	71.3	148	139	94.3	170	87	51.3	38.5
40-44	282	207	73.6	142	134	94.1	140	73	52.6	35.4
45-49	227	167	73.7	116	109	93.9	110	58	52.4	34.6
50-54	203	149	73.7	112	103	92.5	91	46	50.6	30.8
55-59	128	92	71.6	67	61	90.4	61	31	50.7	33.6
60+	381	192	50.5	193	133	69.1	188	59	31.5	30.8
All	7,501	2,484	33.1	3,674	1,511	41.1	3,828	973	25.4	39.2
15+	3,912	2,484	63.5	1,888	1,511	80.0	2,025	973	48.0	39.2

Notes:

a   Per centage of total population that is economically active.

b   Per centage of economically active population that is female.

c   Persons ages 14 years or below are not enumerated in the labour force.

Source: ILO, **Year Book of Labour Statistics**, 1986, p. 19 (Geneva, ILO)

female <u>share</u> of the economically active population -- that is, the per centage of all economically active persons who are women -- falls from slightly over one-half at the youngest ages to less than one-third at the older ages (column 10). Considering all ages combined, women in Zimbabwe constitute almost <u>40 per cent</u> of the country's total labour force as enumerated here.

These figures bring into sharp relief the critical importance of women's economic contributions in every age group to the welfare of the nation, their communities, and their families. Of every ten economically active persons in Zimbabwe, four are women. Economic policies and programmes affecting rural and urban labor markets will clearly have a <u>direct</u> impact on women as well as an indirect impact through male workers in the household (if any). A key question that arises in the context of these observations is the extent to which women workers earn lower wages, on average, and lower returns to self-employment in agriculture or in small-scale industry and services than men do.

The information in Table 2 on the population as a whole includes other information of relevance to planners as well. Three points are illustrated here.

First, the high recorded rate of female labour force participation -- 48 per cent of women aged 15 or more -- reduces the dependency burden on the economically active population (i.e., the <u>dependency ratio</u>). Considering the age distribution alone, there are 112 "dependents" below age 15 and above age 59 for every 100 "working age" adults aged 15 to 59 (3970/3531 x 100; column 1). (This calculation is based on the dubious but typical assumption that all persons above 60 and below 15 are inactive.) Incorporating economic activity (as measured here) into the calculations, there are 202 "inactive" persons of all ages for every 100 economically active persons. (5017/2484 x 100; cols. 1 and 2) In other words, every economically active person supports an average of two other persons. The dependency burden appears high here, primarily because of the high birth rate which causes almost one-half of the total population to be under age 15. But what if the adult female labour force participation rate were half what it is, that is, only 24 per cent instead of 48 per cent? In that case there would be 276 "inactive" persons of all ages for every 100 workers, a dependency burden of almost three to one. The implications of these differing dependency ratios for the welfare of the population should be clear: high rates of female labour force participation reduce the ratios of dependents to workers and raise per capita incomes. Additional research could identify specific socioeconomic groups in which the dependency ratios are highest, and thus of greatest concern.

Given that male labour force participation rates do not vary significantly from country to country, especially within the prime working years, it is hence the <u>female</u> activity rates that are the major determinants of the economic dependency burden within a given age structure. This can be illustrated by data from Burundi, a country with a very high reported adult female participation rate of 95 per cent. Because of this, Burundi has only 107 "inactive" persons of all ages to every 100 "active" persons 15-59 years of age as compared with the ratio of 202 for Zimbabwe. Both countries have approximately the same per centage of their populations in the age group of 15-59 years, however (51 per cent in Burundi and 47 per cent in Zimbabwe).

Second, the population census of Zimbabwe shows an average of 2.3 children under age 15 for every woman of child-bearing years aged 15 to 44 (i.e., the child-woman ratio). Assuming accurate counts of children and adults, this figure provides a rough idea of women's child-rearing responsibilities averaged over the working years. Note, however, that the child-woman ratio includes women who have not yet begun or are in the early stages of child-bearing as well as those who have completed their family size. It does not measure total fertility (an estimate of the average number of live births per woman over the entire reproductive period), which is much higher. In fact, the total fertility rate for Zimbabwe in 1985 was about 6.6 births per woman (Kent and Haub, 1985). These high fertility levels in the face of high female labour force participation (much of it in agriculture) attest to the double burden of production and reproduction that most women carry. Appropriate policies to help alleviate this double burden would include widespread availability of safe and effective family planning services and the provision of child care in the workplace, where feasible.

Third, calculation of the sex ratio for all ages identifies 96 males for every 100 females in Zimbabwe. But the ratio varies markedly by age. There are only 88 men for every 100 women aged 15 to 39, for example, and only 80 men for every 100 women aged 20 to 24. These figures reflect a strong pattern of sex-selective emigration from Zimbabwe at the young adult years which may intensify the demand for female labour and the economic burdens of women, especially in agriculture. Policy relevant research could identify the impact of male emigration on farm output and on household economies. Policies to maintain or increase agricultural production in the absence of working age males, for example, could require special interventions to support women farmers such as direct access to credit on their own behalf, full-fledged membership in farmers' associations, assistance with transport and marketing, and preferential access to tractor services or other essential farm inputs (Palmer, 1985b:71).

2. Regional contrasts in activity profiles

How typical is the Zimbabwe case? Figure 1 compares seven world regions according to the activity rates of their male and female populations in each age group. The rates are based on the ILO estimates for 1980 described above.

One remarkable feature of Figure 1 is the homogeneity of the male activity profiles for the seven regions, all of which are included within the boundaries of "high male" and "low male" rates

Figure 1. Female and male activity rates by age and region, 1980
(ILO estimates)

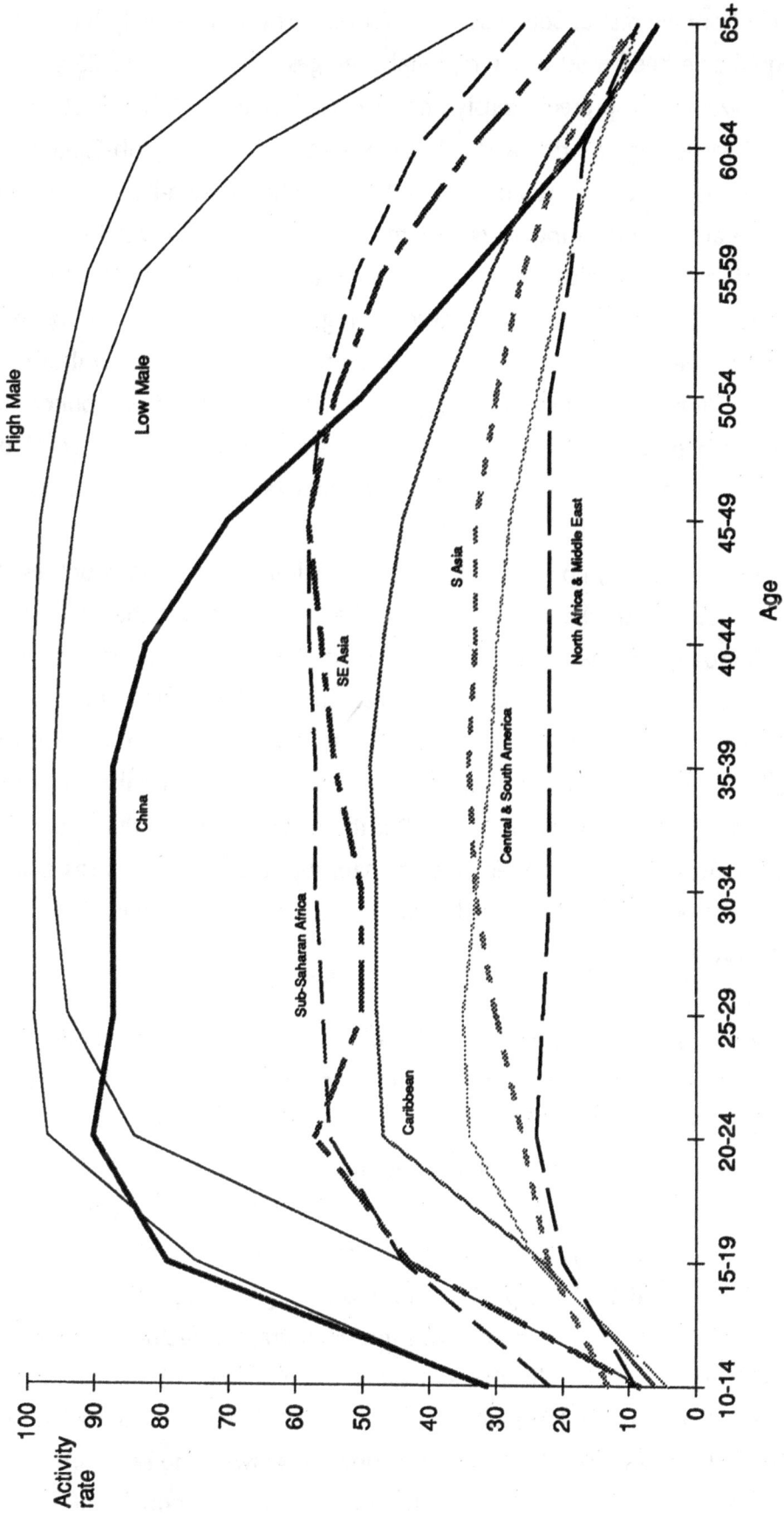

Note: "High male" and "low male" lines represent the regions with the highest and lowest male activity rates for each age category.

Source: ILO, **Economically Active Population, Estimates and Projections, 1950-2025**,1986, Vol.V, Table 2.

at the top of the diagram, compared with the diversity of the female profiles. China, which is drawn separately from the rest of Southeast and East Asia, shows extremely high activity rates for women that equal or exceed most of the regional averages for males up to 25 years of age. The rates for Chinese women drop precipitously after age 40, however. In contrast, activity rates for women in other world regions rise and fall by age more slowly. Sub-Saharan African and Southeast and East Asian women are characterized here by a medium-high activity profile across the prime working and child-bearing years. Women in the Caribbean and South Asia occupy an intermediate position, while those of Central and South America and North Africa and the Middle East have a low activity profile. These aggregate figures of course conceal significant variations among countries as well as within countries, the latter based on rural-urban differences, other geographical differences, and on ethnicity, caste, and class. Such pronounced variability of female labour force participation requires special sensitivity on the part of planners for understanding the determinants and consequences of contrasting levels and trends.

It is important to stress, however, that the ILO estimates for some countries are based on incomplete or biased census data, or on models that do not reflect the full extent of female participation. Virtually all men between the ages of 25 and 50 appear to be counted as economically active regardless of regional contrasts in social and economic conditions. The extent to which differences in the estimated activity rates of women from one region to another (or from one country to another) are due to flawed data or models rather than to real variations in women's work cannot be easily ascertained. But there is little doubt that women's economic activity is systematically under-reported due to inappropriate questionnaires and inconsistent application of the internationally accepted definition of labour force activity. These issues are reviewed in Section III.

Apart from measurement error, a number of factors shape the economic activity profiles of women compared with men in each country and region. These factors have been extensively reviewed elsewhere (e.g., Boserup, 1970, 1975; Durand, 1975; Standing, 1978). Here we may simply refer to the brief discussion of factors determining labour supply and labour demand in earlier papers in this series (Farooq, 1985; Uthoff and Pernia, 1986). These include demographic factors such as fertility, mortality, and internal and international migration, which determine the size and age-sex composition of the population; and a range of economic, social, and cultural factors that interact with one another and with the demographic factors to determine age- and sex-specific activity rates and thus the size and age-sex composition of the labour force. Cultural attitudes about women's work outside the home and the availability of alternative forms of child-care are also important here, as are the rate of economic growth, the structure of the economy, the level and type of industrialisation, factor prices and the choice of technology, and consumption patterns and income distribution. Each of the factors listed above that influences the overall supply of and demand for labour in each society -- that is, the availability of human resources and the effectiveness with which they are utilised -- will affect male and female populations differently. In general, female labour force participation is more responsive to changes in these factors than is male labour force participation. Each factor will also have a differential impact on activity rates according to age, ethnicity, class, education, caste, geographical location, and other relevant characteristics of major population subgroups. Characteristics of the labour force cannot be fully understood without disaggregation of this type.

3. Time trends in male and female participation

Many developing countries have not taken periodic censuses or surveys permitting the analysis of changes in activity rates by age and sex over time. The ILO estimates for the period from 1950 to 1980 suggest that aggregate activity rates for men have declined in all regions. The reason for this is the shrinkage of male labour force participation at younger ages, as schooling is extended, and at older ages, as men retire earlier. Male rates may decline very slightly during the prime working years, but they generally remain close to 100 per cent. For women, however, trends are inconsistent among regions and even among countries within regions. Although women share with men the tendency for activity rates to decline somewhat over time at younger and older ages, they differ substantially in their trends during the middle years.

Figure 2 indicates changes from 1950 to 1980 in male and female activity rates at ages 30 to 34 for seven world regions according to ILO estimates. Note that whereas rates for men hover between about 96 and 99 per cent throughout the three decades in all regions, those for women are characterised by contrasting levels and trends. The very high rates for Chinese women have risen further since 1950, according to these estimates, while the very low average rates for North African and Middle Eastern women have fallen further. The relatively low rates for women in Central and South America and in the Caribbean are estimated to have climbed sharply, especially from 1970 to 1980, while the high rates for women in the sub-Saharan African region are estimated to have dropped slightly. Women in Southeast and East Asia (excluding China) are estimated to have become more active over time but in South Asia to have become less active. While these trends may represent true variations over time in activity rates, it is important to remember that many are undoubtedly affected by inaccuracies in measuring the female labour force. For example, the reported activity rates for women ages 5 years and above in the last three Indian censuses, which shifted from 31 to 16 per cent and then to 24 per cent, could not have been due to underlying changes in employment patterns (Sinha, 1982).

The implications of these observations for the projection of the size and structure of the labour force are profound. Clearly, quite different sets of equations based on different assumptions are required for male and female workers (Sehgal, 1986). Activity rates for females are less predictable than those for males. They are more responsive than male rates to changes in

Figure 2. Trends in female and male activity rates at ages 30-34, 1950-1980, by region (ILO estimates)

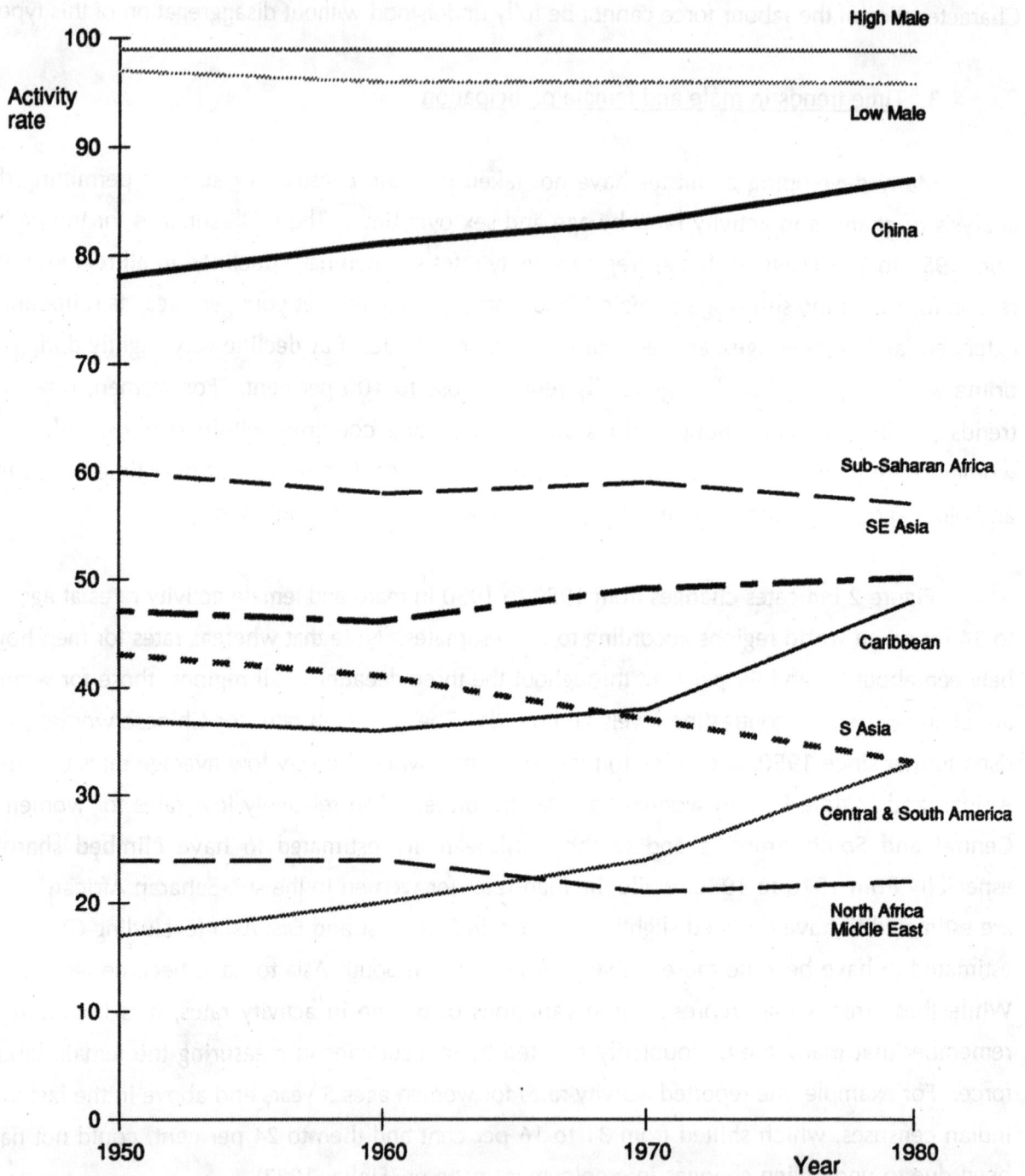

Note: "High male" and "low male" lines represent the regions with the highest and lowest male activity rates for each age category. The lines with regional labels represent female activity rates.

Source: ILO, **Economically Active Population, Estimates and Projections, 1950-2025**, 1986, Vol.V, Table2.

the factors affecting labour supply and demand noted above, such as changing patterns of economic growth, occupational distribution, family formation and dissolution, and shifting social attitudes. Female activity rates are also more likely to be affected by measurement inaccuracies.

The accuracy of labour force forecasts for each country thus depends heavily on what assumptions are made about changes in women's roles. The direction of change predicted in the ILO projections to the year 2025 is mixed. In some regions the female work-force is projected to grow faster than the male work-force throughout the entire period; in others, slower. In some regions it is projected to grow faster initially and then slower; in others, slower and then faster. Regardless of the accuracy of these forecasts, many countries will experience marked changes in the sex composition of the labour force over the next several decades. This has important implications for development planning as male and female workers tend to be concentrated in particular occupations and sectors of the economy (see below). It could imply a need to train women (and men) for nontraditional occupations. New or expanded government services and programmes may also be required in other areas such as credit, extension services, and marketing, in order to prevent the displacement of women workers or a decline in their conditions of work (Ahmed, 1987). Projected growth of the female labour force may require intensified efforts to ensure adequate child care and to eliminate sex discrimination in hirign, promotion, and wages.

B. Occupational Distributions of Male and Female Workers

Population censuses commonly classify the economically active population according to both occupation and industry. In publications such as the **Year Book of Labour Statistics**, occupations and industries are grouped into nine categories (one-digit census codes). Occupations are identified in greater detail in the tabulations of census and survey results in each country using two-digit or three-digit coding systems.

The tendency for women to be concentrated in particular occupations and in particular sectors of the economy is universal. But the nature and the degree of occupational segregation based on gender differ significantly from one country to the next according to economic, social, and demographic circumstances and to the cultural sex stereotyping of particular occupations, among other factors. Consider, for example, a typical illustration based on published tabulations of the distribution of male and female workers across major occupational classifications. The information on the economically active population in Table 3 is based on the 1980 population census of Malaysia. Column 7 has been added to emphasise certain points.

Table 3. Economically active population by occupation and sex,
Malaysia population census, 1980 (numbers in thousands)

Occupation (major group)	Total (1)	% (2)	Males (3)	% (4)	Females (5)	% (6)	Female share of econ. active pop. (%) (7)
0-1 Professional, technical, and related workers	303.1	6.2	187.2	5.7	115.9	7.0	38.2
2 Administrative and managerial	44.3	0.9	40.7	1.2	3.7	0.2	8.4
3 Clerical and related workers	349.8	7.1	198.4	6.1	151.3	9.1	43.2
4 Sales workers	398.4	8.1	299.8	9.2	98.6	5.9	24.7
5 Service workers	383.4	7.7	260.5	8.0	122.9	7.4	32.0
6 Agriculture, animal husbandry, forestry, hunters, fishermen	1,672.9	34.0	1,040.9	31.9	632.0	38.1	37.8
7-9 Production and related workers, transport equip. operators, and laborers	1,116.7	22.7	875.8	26.8	240.9	14.5	21.6
X Workers not classified by occ.	324.5	6.6	189.4	5.8	135.1	8.1	41.6
- Unemployed persons not previously employed	72.9	1.5	42.5	1.3	30.3	1.8	41.6
- Unemployed persons previously employed	257.7	5.2	130.6	4.0	127.2	7.7	49.4
Total	4,923.8	100.0	3,265.8	100.0	1,657.9	100.0	33.7

Source: ILO, **Year Book of Labour Statistics**, 1986, p. 140 (Geneva, ILO).

1. Occupational segregation of female workers: an Asian example

Of the almost 5 million persons in the Malaysian labour force in 1980, 34 per cent were employed in agricultural occupations and almost 23 per cent in production and related occupations (column 2). Note that female workers were much more likely than male workers to be employed in agriculture, however, and much less likely to be employed in production and related occupations (columns 4 and 6). In addition, a higher proportion of the female than male labour force was employed in professional and clerical occupations, and a lower proportion in administrative/managerial, sales, and service occupations. Table 3 also reveals that economically active women are more likely than men to be unemployed.

The tabulations described above allow direct comparisons of the occupational distributions of the male and female work force. In contrast, column 7 shows the percentages of all workers in each occupation who are women, that is, the female share of the economically active population in each major occupational group. Overall, women comprise one-third of the total labour force. Using this figure as a base, we see at a glance that women are concentrated in varying degrees among clerical, professional and technical, and agricultural workers and among the unclassified and unemployed. Women are relatively underrepresented in varying degrees among administrative and managerial workers, sales workers, and production workers.

These calculations offer a quick snapshot of the nature and degree of sex segregation across major occupational groups. They also raise questions of policy relevance. Extreme concentrations of men or women in particular occupations (and their virtual exclusion from others) signify the existence of labour market barriers and inflexibility, and therefore a sub-optimal use of human resources. Moreover, such concentrations reflect patterns of unequal access of females and males to education and training at different levels and of different types, as well as women's comparative disadvantage in competing for full-time year-round work because of child-care and other family obligations. Each of these disadvantages is amenable to correction through policy intervention.

It is also important to recognise that changes in the demand for labour in particular occupations will have a different impact on women than on men. In Bangladesh, for example, the rapid growth of mechanised rice milling following on the heels of rural electrification has led to the displacement of an estimated 3.5 to 5 million days of female labour per year (Ahmed, 1987:24). Women from landless or near landless households had been responsible for 86 per cent of all employment in rice processing, specialising in husking by the traditional dheki. In contrast, the jobs created in the new automated or semi-automated mills were almost exclusively male. In the absence of alternative sources of income for rural women, the inflexibility of labour market barriers has caused intensified impoverishment of women (many of them from female-

them from female-headed households) who had formerly relied on this source of employment. This is a good example of where a planner might step in with programmes designed to offer credit, skills training, intermediate technology, or some other intervention for displaced women workers in order to prevent drastic reductions in household incomes.

2. Regional contrasts in sex segregation

The ILO estimates permit comparisons of the sectoral distribution of female and male workers for all countries across agricultural, industrial, and service occupations. Table 4 presents estimates for 1980 for seven regions in the developing world. According to these figures, female workers are more likely than male workers to be concentrated in agriculture in sub-Saharan Africa, North Africa and the Middle East, and Asia, and less likely to be concentrated in agriculture in Central and South America and the Caribbean. Women workers are less likely than men to be in industrial occupations in all seven regions. Within the service sector the situation is mixed, with wide regional differences. In general, male workers are spread more evenly across the three sectors -- that is, they are more diversified occupationally -- than are women workers.

The tendency for women to be concentrated within particular sectors of the economy is quickly apparent in the calculations of the female share of the economically active population in the total labour force and within each sector. Also clear are the sharp contrasts among world regions in the profiles of concentration. According to Figure 3, women's share of total employment ranges from over 40 per cent in Eastern Africa and in East Asia (excluding China) to under 15 per cent in Northern Africa. The shape of the diagrams highlights the sectors in which women are overrepresented or underrepresented in comparison with their share of total employment. The flat profile of Northern Africa, for example, reflects a universally low female share of employment in all three sectors and thus a low degree of concentration, as estimated here. (Female unpaid family workers employed in agriculture have been systematically excluded, by definition, in the censuses of some North African countries, however.) Similarly, the relatively flat profile of Southeast Asia reflects a universally high female share of employment in all three sectors and a low degree of concentration. In contrast, the profiles for other regions are marked by sometimes sharp peaks and troughs reflecting strong propensities for sex segregation within major sectors of the economy.

It is important to note that the degree of occupational segregation by sex that one observes in the reported statistics is related to the detail of the occupational categories being considered. The finer the occupational distribution (i.e., the more occupations identified), the greater the sex segregation tends to be (Anker and Hein, 1986:96-102). For example, data from around the world for the broad category of professional, technical and related workers show that

Table 4. Distribution of male and female workers by economic sector and region, 1980
(per centage of total male and female labour force employed in each sector)

Region	Males			Females		
	Agriculture (1)	Industry (2)	Services (3)	Agriculture (4)	Industry (5)	Services (6)
Sub-Saharan Africa	58.2	19.5	22.2	69.2	6.3	24.5
North Africa, Middle East	42.4	22.5	35.2	59.8	13.6	26.6
South Asia	65.1	13.9	21.0	77.1	11.3	11.6
Southeast, East Asia	44.9	23.6	31.4	51.4	18.8	29.9
China	71.0	15.5	13.5	78.5	12.0	9.5
Caribbean	40.4	24.4	35.3	25.5	14.2	60.3
Central, South America	34.3	30.0	35.6	11.4	21.0	67.7

Source: ILO, **Economically Active Population, Estimates and Projections, 1950-2025**, 1986, Vol. V, Table 3.

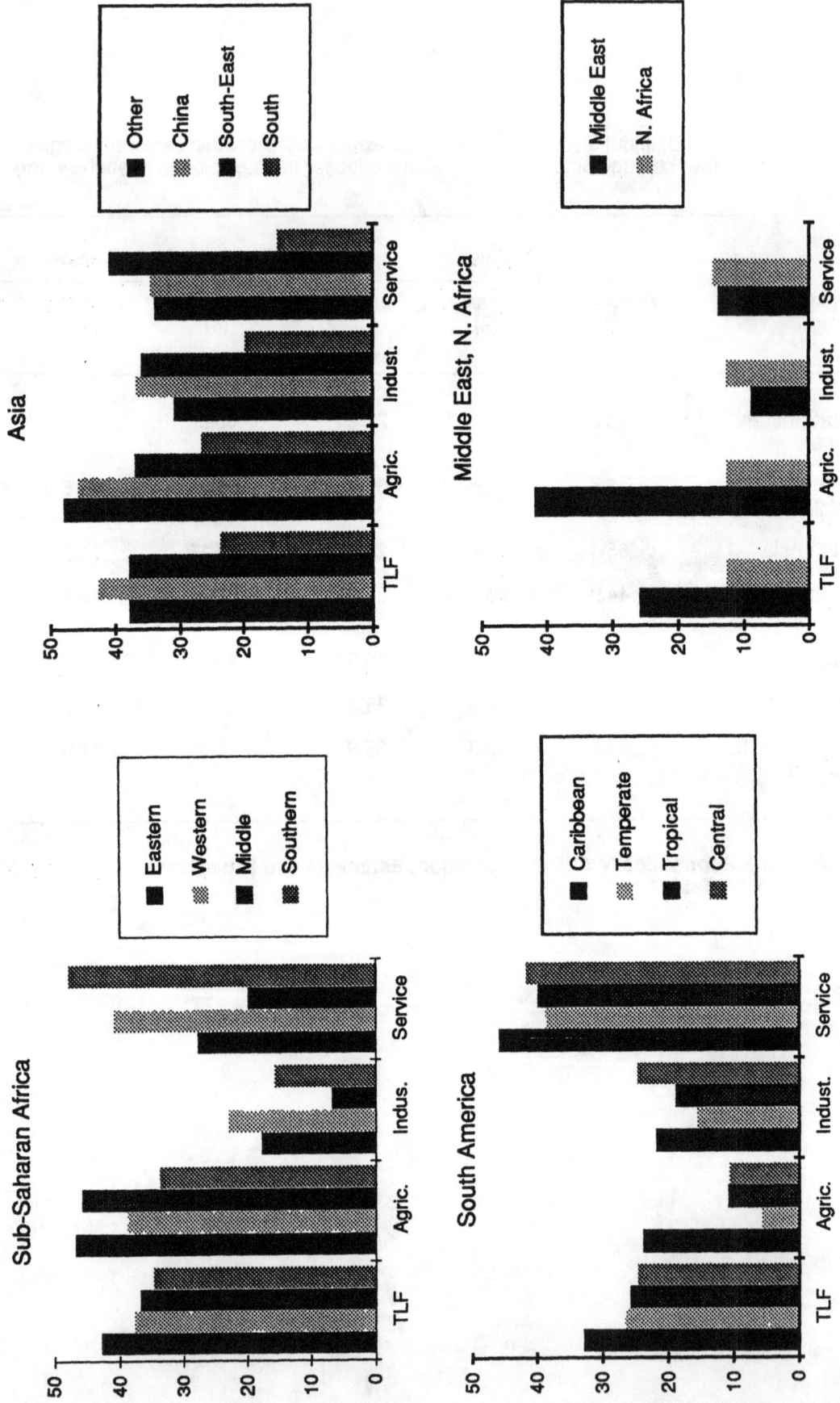

Figure 3. Female share (%) of total labour force by economic sector and region, 1980 (ILO estimates)

Asia

Sub-Saharan Africa

Middle East, N. Africa

South America

Source: ILO, Economically Active Population, Estimates and Projections, 1950-2025 , 1986, Vol. V, Table 3.

the relatively high per centage of women reported in professional occupations is due almost entirely to their concentration in only two occupations: teaching (primary or secondary school) and nursing.

There is little that is "natural" about the sex typing of particular occupations such as primary school teaching or bus driving. Indeed, variations from one country to another in what is considered men's or women's work are sometimes dramatic. Sex segregation is the product primarily of social beliefs about appropriate male and female roles that are perpetuated in differential socialisation, in differential education and training, and in discriminatory hiring and promotion practices. Nor is most occupational sex typing as resistant to change as one might suppose. More and more, research is showing that sex segregation patterns in labour markets that are cultural in origin break down easily in the face of changes in labour demand (Buvinic, 1983:19). They can also be challenged by policies requiring employers to examine their hiring and promotion practices for evidence of sex discrimination and, if necessary, to adopt affirmative action procedures. Such policies help to correct previous patterns of under-utilisation and mis-utilisation of human resources.

C. The Employment Status of Male and Female Workers

Population censuses and labour force surveys typically classify the economically active population not only by occupation and industry but also by three categories of employment status: employees, employers and own-account workers, and unpaid family workers. Classifications of this type reveal interesting patterns of sex segregation in the labour force according to the conditions of work.

In general, women are far more likely than men to be unpaid family workers and less likely to be employees or own-account workers (see Appendix Table A). This is especially true of the agricultural sector, where women often work without pay on family holdings. A typical case is Sri Lanka. According to the 1981 census, 27 per cent of female workers in agriculture were unpaid family workers but only 14 per cent of male agricultural workers were unpaid family workers. In the non-agricultural labour force, 6 per cent of female workers were unpaid family workers as compared with 2 per cent of male workers. The implications of this observation are that, in general, women in the labour force are less likely than men to be earning an income in cash or kind. Instead, unpaid family workers depend on other family members for a share of the income (if any) their labour has generated. The extent to which women (and other non-earning household members such as children) actually share in the benefits of incomes accruing to males depends on complex cultural conditions unique to each setting. Moreover, an emerging research literature suggests that incomes earned by women are more likely to go toward filling the basic human needs of children and other household members than are incomes earned by men. Thus, the question of who in the household has direct access to earnings rather than indirect (i.e., through dependence on another person) can be highly relevant in ascertaining the wellbeing of particular categories of household members.

Table 5, which is based on the 1981 population census of Guatemala, summarises a standard format of data on the economically active population classified by employment status obtained from the **Year Book of Labour Statistics**. Only the totals are shown here; in the original, the employment status of workers is shown for each of the major occupational groups.

Column 4 shows that of the 1,439 thousand economically active males in Guatemala, 46 per cent were employers and own-account workers and 44 per cent were employees. Among women only 24 per cent were employers or own-account workers and 67 per cent were employees. The striking over-representation of women among paid employees compared with their representation in the labour force as a whole is somewhat unusual for a developing country (Anker and Hein 1986:73). (Note, however, that despite this over-representation only one of every five employees was female.) Also unusual in this example is the lower per centage of women than men who were unpaid family workers.

How is information such as this useful to planners? Among other things, it highlights the differential access of women and men to wage-paying employment and to self-employment -- that is, to jobs characterised by sharply different working conditions (e.g., place of work, regularity of hours, bargaining power, worker control over the labour process) and different levels and security of incomes and other benefits. It also reveals the extent to which women have direct access to income-earning opportunities as compared with labouring without pay in a family enterprise. When tabulated for every occupation, the break-downs by employment status are especially revealing. For in this way one can identify prevailing patterns of self-employment and wage-employment of women compared with men within each occupational category. Such information is especially useful for designing policies and programmes aimed at raising the productivity of women's self-employment, which is almost always under-capitalised compared with men's and consequently results in low productivity and low returns to labour.

Table 5. Economically active population by employment status and sex,
Guatemala population census, 1981
(numbers in thousands)

Employment status	Total (1)	% (2)	Males (3)	% (4)	Females (5)	% (6)	Female share of econ. active pop. (7)
Employers and own-account workers	715.7	42.5	657.9	45.7	57.8	23.6	8.1
Employees	795.3	47.2	631.7	43.9	163.5	66.7	20.6
Unpaid family workers	114.2	6.8	105.5	7.3	8.8	3.6	7.7
Not classifiable by status	58.6	3.5	43.5	3.0	15.1	6.2	25.8
Total	1,683.8	100.0	1,438.6	100.0	245.2	100.0	14.6

Source: ILO, **Year Book of Labour Statistics**, 1985, pp. 126-7 (Geneva, ILO).

III. COUNTING WOMEN IN THE LABOUR FORCE:
INCONSISTENCIES AND POSSIBILITIES

The importance of female labour force participation for understanding women's economic contributions to development cannot be denied. But how accurate are official figures on the size and composition of the labour force? How much of the geographical and temporal variations in female labour force participation reported in the previous section are due to differences in enumeration procedures -- or in the models on which estimates are based -- rather than to differences in real conditions? The answer to both questions, of course, is "it depends". The results of repeated population censuses in some developing countries inspire confidence because of their apparent consistency; in others they raise serious doubts because of obvious discrepancies. Even those that are consistent from one census to the next, however, may be consistently biased in their undercounting of certain categories of workers such as persons working without pay on agricultural holdings.

Problems of definition and procedure plague the collection of labour force statistics in almost all situations, in industrialised and developing countries alike, for young and old, male and female. Yet women (and children) are disproportionately undercounted as workers in most population censuses of developing countries for a number of reasons. Some relate to the definitions of economic activity proposed in international guidelines, as described below. Others relate to the selective application of these guidelines, for example when certain activities such as animal husbandry are not considered as labour force activity; when questions are worded in ways that encourage women to report themselves as housewives even if they work for pay; or when interviewers simply assume that wives are not economically active based on inaccurate societal stereotypes.

This section begins by illustrating some of the more obvious discrepancies in official labour force statistics obtained from population censuses and other sources. We follow this with a critique of the way in which the concept of economic activity has been defined and interpreted and the way in which questions about economic activity have often been asked. Suggestions are made throughout on how to reduce the underenumeration of women in the labour force and improve the comparability of results. Our purpose in dwelling on this topic at such length is to stress the importance of obtaining accurate data on female as well as male employment patterns as a precondition both for understanding the social and economic implications of the prevailing sexual division of labour in each country, and for planning for the full integration of women in national development efforts.

A. Missing Persons: Discrepancies in Official Statistics and the Undercounting of Women Workers

In some countries, unpaid family workers -- especially females in agriculture -- are systematically excluded from the economically active population. This results in a consistent undercount of the agricultural labour force as a whole as well as an underestimate of the proportion of all agricultural workers who are women. In other countries, women appear and disappear in startling fashion from one census or survey to the next. The census of Algeria, for example, counted 981 thousand women in agricultural occupations in 1954 (37 per cent of the total farm labour force) but only 23 thousand in 1966 (2 per cent of the total). A footnote to the 1966 census noted that the enumerated economically active population excluded 1.2 million females who were "mainly occupied in agriculture." If they had been included, then the total agricultural work force would have been 2. 5 million persons rather than the reported 1.3 million and the female share of the total would have been 49 per cent rather than the reported 2 per cent.

Many other illustrations can be cited from the **Year Book of Labour Statistics** and from other sources (e.g., see Durand 1975:239-249). Because of changes in the definition of economic activity and the way questions were asked, the census of India counted 49 million women in agricultural occupations in 1961 but only 26 million in 1971, a drop in the female share of the total from 36 to 20 per cent. By 1981 the figure had risen to 36 million, or a 24 per cent female share. In Brazil, the 1950 census counted 761 thousand women in the farm labour force, or 7 per cent of all agricultural workers. A national survey in 1976 raised this figure to 3 million, or 21 per cent of the work force.   And in Egypt, two successive national labour force surveys produced almost identical results for the male labour force but large differences in the female labour force. These surveys counted 3,805 thousand male workers in agriculture in 1982 and 3,848 thousand in 1983. But the same surveys counted only 69 thousand female farm workers in 1982 compared with 794 thousand in 1983, representing female shares of 2 and 17 per cent. The 2 per cent figure is consistent with earlier population censuses. But the 17 per cent figure is more consistent with a detailed rural labour record survey which found that one-quarter of all non-domestic productive work in farm households was done by women, and with more recent time-use surveys that found even higher female contributions (Dixon 1982:540). Indeed, this observed increase in the number of female agricultural workers between the 1982 and 1983 national labour force surveys in Egypt is due to a conscious effort of the Egyptian statistical office to enumerate such workers in the 1983 survey by specifying in the interviewer instructions the need to include each activity.

It would be difficult to underestimate the importance of these differences to planners of agricultural development and rural employment policies and programmes. Is there a labour shortage in Egyptian agriculture, for example, which could be alleviated by policies favouring more rapid mechanisation, as some planners contend, or is there a labour surplus? Are women (and children) largely a dispensable workforce or are they critical to the production effort -- especially at times of peak season demand? Has the outmigration of rural males in search of work elsewhere drawn additional women into farm labour, or has the burden increased for women who have always worked in this capacity? How do these patterns differ according to the size of the holding, the cropping pattern, or the region of the country? How does the resulting sexual division of labour affect agricultural productivity? All of these questions, and more, require accurate data that includes a full counting of female labour inputs.

Contradictory results such as those cited above make it very difficult to understand the composition of the work force in some countries and how it may be changing. In addition, differences in definitions and data collection methods from one country to the next complicate attempts to compare activity rates across countries and regions. In some cases comparisons may be useless.

Evidence suggests that inconsistencies in the enumeration of the economically active population are most likely to appear among women, particularly among those employed in agriculture where unpaid work is most common. Table 6 compares the economic activity rates of women and men based on population censuses and specialised household surveys in Panama, Bolivia, and Brazil. Note that there is a high degree of consistency between the censuses and surveys in the activity rates obtained for men in both urban and rural areas (column 3). For women, however, the surveys obtained activity rates up to three times higher than the censuses (column 6). Disparities between the two sources for women are most pronounced among rural populations and agricultural workers and least pronounced in urban areas and non-agricultural occupations. In essence, it appears that men in their prime working years are almost always counted as economically active regardless of the definitions or data collection procedures used. But whether women (and children) are counted as economically active or not depends on a number of complex methodological issues, some of which are addressed below.

Table 6. Comparison of male and female activity rates at ages 30 to 39 from population censuses and household surveys: Panama, Bolivia, and Brazil

Place and year	Male Rates			Female Rates		
	Census (C) (1)	Survey (S) (2)	S/C (3)	Census (C) (4)	Survey (S) (5)	S/C (6)
Panama 1970a						
Metropolitan area	96.6	99.2	1.03	44.9	56.2	1.25
Rest of country	98.1	99.2	1.01	21.7	24.9	1.15
Bolivia 1975-76b						
Capital city	98.3	97.3	0.99	35.9	36.8	1.03
Other urban areas	98.0	97.7	1.00	32.9	30.6	0.93
Rural areas	99.0	98.8	1.00	15.7	35.0	2.23
Sao Paulo, Brazil 1970c						
Nonagricultural workers	75.7	77.4	1.02	21.4	24.8	1.16
Agricultural workers	19.7	19.7	1.00	1.2	4.2	3.50

Notes:

a   1970 Population Census and 1970 Labour Force Survey.

b   1976 Population Census and 1975 National Demographic Survey.

c   1970 Population Census and 1970 Household Survey of State of Sao Paulo; Ages 35 to 44.

Source: Recchini de Lattes and Wainerman, 1982, pages 15, 21, 25.

B. What is Economic Activity? The Search for an Adequate Definition

Concepts and methods of reckoning labour force participation based on contemporary Western experience have proven inadequate when applied to developing countries, where workers are more likely than those in more industrialised countries to be self-employed or unpaid family workers rather than wage earners, to work seasonally rather than year-round, to be under-employed rather than formally unemployed, and to engage in multiple economic activities. Moreover, the boundary between domestic production for the household's own consumption and economic activity for sale or exchange is less clearly drawn in developing countries, especially in rural areas, and especially among women.

These difficulties are compounded in the agricultural sector, where subsistence-oriented farmers may sell very little of their produce, where unpaid labour on their own land may alternate with wage labour on another's, where children may regularly tend small animals or women tend kitchen gardens or process crops in their compounds but not work in the fields, and where trade or crafts are added to agricultural work in a seasonal mix of household activities. Indeed, the conceptual distinctions between persons who are economically active and inactive, and between agricultural and non-agricultural occupations, often become hopelessly blurred, particularly in the case of women. In the discussion that follows we propose a method for creating multiple definitions of labour force activity that help to resolve some of these methodological dilemmas.

1. International standard definitions

Conventional labour force definitions have been heavily criticised for their tendency to omit much of the productive work that women do. Such omissions derive in part from the emphasis on <u>paid</u> production which consequently devalues subsistence production, and in part from an apparent gender bias in drawing the line between subsistence production <u>outside</u> the home and the production of goods and services <u>inside</u> the home. In the latter case, the dividing line seems to be drawn only partly on the basis of some intrinsic characteristic of the activity itself, and partly at the point at which it is most likely to be done by "housewives".

In 1982 the Thirteenth International Conference of Labour Statisticians recommended a new definition of the economically active population (and of under-employment and unemployment). The labour force definition of 1954 had included "Persons who perform some work <u>for pay or profit</u>" (emphasis added) during a specified brief period. The definition was expanded in 1966 to include "All persons of either sex who furnish the supply of labour for the production of <u>economic goods and services</u>" (ILO, 1976). The latest international standard clarifies what is to be considered "economic". The economically active population includes "all persons of either sex who furnish the supply of labour for the production of economic goods and services <u>as defined by the United Nations systems of national accounts and balances</u>" (Anker, 1983; ILO, 1983). The new definition allows for the measurement of both the <u>currently active</u> population measured in relation to a short reference period such as one week or one day (i.e., the standard "labour force" concept) and the <u>usually active</u> population measured in relation to a long reference period such as a season or a year (i.e., the standard "gainfully employed" concept).

What constitutes "economic goods and services" as defined in the systems of national income accounts? All work for pay or in anticipation of profit would clearly be included. In principle many activities oriented toward own consumption should also be included, such as subsistence agriculture, home construction and improvement, milking animals, and processing food (UN, 1968). The new standard declares that "... the production of economic goods and services should include <u>all production and processing of primary products</u>, whether for the market, for barter or <u>for own consumption</u>" (emphasis added). According to this concept, most of the subsistence-oriented production and processing (but not housework) that women do in developing countries should be incorporated into the definition of economic activity. The following is a schematic representation (ILO, 1983:2).

Production and processing of	Production of economic goods and services for		
	market only	market and own consumption	own consumption only
Primary products[a]	LF	LF	LF[b]
Other products	LF	LF	

LF indicates that activity is to be included in the labour force.
[a] Products from agriculture, hunting, forestry, fishing, mining and quarrying.
[b] Only processing of primary commodities by the producers of these commodities is included. The processing of purchased primary commodities such as fish, grains, or wood for home consumption is excluded.

In practice, however, many countries do not consider as "economic" such activities as gathering wild foods, fuel or water, processing crops, raising a few chickens or keeping a kitchen garden. Indeed, the boundary between labour force ("economic") and non labour force (i.e., "non-economic") activity is often arbitrary. National practices on the inclusion in national income statistics of the value of subsistence activities (the basis for labour force definitions) vary considerably. An investigation of the accounting systems of 70 developing countries revealed that 71 per cent reportedly included the imputed value of forestry activities (including gathering fruits or thatching grass, cutting firewood, etc.); 50 per cent the value of handicraft production; 39 per cent food processing; and 7 per cent water carrying (Blades, 1975). Similar variation is found in labour force statistics. Fiji, for example, considers the tending of poultry to be a labour force activity only if the worker is raising at least ten chickens (Blacker, 1978).

Some critics might contend that including all subsistence-oriented production and the processing of primary products dilutes the concept of economic activity, thus weakening its usefulness as an indicator of development processes. Yet there are good arguments to be made for the inclusion of such activities, especially from the perspective of assessing women's contributions. Not only is female labour more likely to be concentrated in the subsistence sector, as hoted previously, but a thriving subsistence sector can make an important contribution to development through the provision of food, clothing, and other necessities of life that improve the health and wellbeing of the population and raise the productivity of labour. Indeed, policies directed toward improving the productivity of subsistence agriculture and related activities could have a significant impact in reducing rural poverty and slowing the flow of migrants to impacted urban areas.

The new international definition of economic activity abolishes the previous stipulation that persons working without pay in a family enterprise be counted in the labour force only if they worked at least one-third of the "normal" working time. In this sense, it treats unpaid family workers the same way as other categories of workers, that is, the same as wage earners and the self-employed. But it adds a new stipulation that is virtually impossible to quantify. The new definition recognises as "working" those who produce solely for their own or their household's consumption <u>only if such production comprises "an important contribution to the total consumption of the household"</u> (ILO, 1983). In practice, most census and survey takers are likely to fall back on an estimate of working time in order to make this decision. The new criterion of "importance" unfortunately leaves the door wide open for the continued underreporting of women's contributions in the subsistence economy. When women engage in a multitude of subsistence activities, each of which takes a small amount of time and contributes a small portion of the household's total consumption, their labour is especially likely to be devalued.

The major problem in the quest for an adequate definition is the attempt to force into a single dichotomy (i.e., whether economically active or not) a complex and fluid mix of behavior with porous activity boundaries and time boundaries. In short, one single definition is not likely to be adequate for all purposes. One solution to this problem is to devise a more flexible system of standard multiple definitions for multiple uses.

2. Needed: multiple definitions for multiple uses

Given the ambiguities and arbitrariness involved in the often artificial distinction between "economic" and "non-economic" activities, some researchers have questioned the appropriateness of making a distinction at all, especially in rural areas. Among the poor in developing countries virtually all adults and most children engage in "economic activities" to help the family meet its basic needs. Much of this is subsistence production. The question is not so much whether men, women and children are or are not economically active, but rather, how many hours they are working, what they are doing, and what returns they gain for their labours. To claim that many persons must be excluded from the labour force simply to retain variability in the statistic belies the actual situation in many parts of the Third World.

There is clearly a need for several measures of the labour force -- measures that also indicate the type (e.g., paid, not paid) and level (part-time, full-time) of activity based on different definitions. Only in this way will it be possible for planners to have accurate and comparable labour force data that are useful for specific purposes. Four definitions are proposed here. Progressing from the least to most inclusive conceptualisation, each provides distinctive information on the labour market and on the various forms of contribution to household and national incomes.

(a) Paid labour force (persons in wage or salary employment for which they are paid in cash or kind). Corresponding closely to the employment status category of "employees" currently in use, this is the most restrictive definition of economic activity. Current measures of the paid labour force are believed to be relatively accurate and thus comparable across countries and over time. Anyone who earns income in cash or kind from wages or salaries within the specified reference period, regardless of hours worked, would typically be included. The value of wages and salaries paid is routinely included in national accounts. This narrow definition of economic activity is useful for planning purposes that focus specifically on job creation or on monitoring wages, working conditions, and job opportunities in wage employment.

(b) Market-oriented labour force (persons in paid employment plus persons engaged in activities on a family farm or in a family enterprise that sells some or all of its products). The latter group includes employers, own-account workers, unpaid family workers in a market-oriented farm or business, and members of a producer co-operative. It would also include persons engaged in related activities that add to the profit of a family enterprise, for example, in animal and poultry husbandry where products such as milk or eggs are sold, or in the preparation of meals for hired labourers, since food and drink are often a form of payment. This intermediate measure of labour force participation captures all economic activity directly connected with the money economy. For data to be comparable across countries and over time, however, the treatment of unpaid family workers in market-oriented activities must be consistent. In principle, all economic exchanges of this type are included in national accounts statistics. The market-oriented definition is particularly useful for policies designed to expand opportunities for self-employment through training, credit, technical assistance, and other support services.

(c) New standard labour force (persons engaged in activities whose products or services should be included in the national income accounts statistics according to United Nations recommendations). This definition of economic activity corresponds to that recommended by the Thirteenth International Conference of Labour Statisticians noted above. Interpreted correctly, it includes persons engaged in the production of goods and services for the market as well as the processing of primary products produced by the household. For example, all tasks associated with primary products such as growing vegetables or raising poultry, caring for livestock, threshing in the home compound, and gathering of wild foods and firewood or fodder for household consumption would be considered labour force activities. This broad definition omits housework, child-rearing, and other activities related to the reproduction of the labour force, however. As noted earlier, raising the productivity of subsistence activities such as irrigation or crop processing is critical to the success of development efforts. It can improve the wellbeing of the population significantly as well as reducing the drudgery of many tasks and releasing workers for other pursuits.

(d) Total labour force (persons engaged in economic activities as defined above, plus those engaged in the production or processing of primary and non-primary products and services for use in the home (e.g., sewing clothes for family members, preserving purchased foods) and other domestic and related activities such as meal preparation (preparing and cooking food, serving food and cleaning up), cleaning the dwelling and its surroundings, care of clothing (laundering, ironing, mending), personal care of other household members, and all shopping related to these tasks. These activities are also "economic" in the broad meaning of the term, i.e., they use the scarce resource of labour to produce goods and services. The distinction between domestic activities that are included in the total labour force, and domestic activities that are not, can be made by applying the "third person" principle: activities are considered to have "economic value" if they could be performed by a paid worker to achieve the same results (Reid, 1934, quoted in Goldschmidt-Clermont, 1987a:5). Cooking a meal or proving child-care thus have economic value, for example, while school attendance, leisure activities, social visiting, religious observances, and participation in various community events do not. This comprehensive concept of economic activity is useful for planning purposes that require a full assessment of the value of goods and services produced by all household members.

The value of such domestic activities is not currently included in systems of national accounts, however, despite indications that they account for approximately 40 to 45 per cent of total labour time and approximately 25 to 50 per cent of measured gross national product in developing countries (Goldschmidt-Clermont, 1987a:58-9). The question of how to attribute economic value to non-market domestic activities is discussed in greater detail in Section IV.D.

An illustration of the type of activities included in each labour force definition is presented in Table 7. The definitions are cumulative from top to bottom and from left to right. One methodological survey in the state of Uttar Pradesh, India, which used an activity schedule to collect information, found that activity rates for women were 13 per cent in the paid labour force, 32 per cent in the market-oriented labour force, and 88 per cent in the new standard international definition. (Anker, Khan and Gupta, 1987:159). Activity rates for the total labour force category, which includes housework, were not calculated. Among women who were counted as economically active within the first three groups, the proportions employed more than half-time rose from 41 per cent within the paid labour force to over 50 per cent within the new standard labour force. The effects of using the four labour force definitions on the resulting activity rates would vary significantly in different settings, of course, and according to the age, sex, ethnicity, and caste or class of the respondent, among other factors.

C. Asking Survey Questions: How To Avoid Biased Results

The ways in which questions about economic activities are asked of respondents in censuses or sample surveys will inevitably shape the answers provided and thus the statistical outcomes. Words such as "employment", "job", "work", or "main activity" mean very different things to different people. The order in which questions are asked, the amount of probing, the time reference period used, the minimum number of hours required for unpaid workers to be included in the labour force, and the assumptions made by interviewers and respondents, all help to determine whether a person will be classified as economically active or not. Each of these factors is a matter of concern in obtaining valid and reliable labour force information.

1. The meaning of "keywords"

Censuses and labour force surveys typically consist of "keyword" questions, that is, questions based on a keyword or phrase embedded in a longer question. For example, the 1961 census of India asked, "Are you working as 'Cultivator', 'Agricultural Labour', working at 'Household Industries' or working under any other category ...?" The 1971 census asked "What is your main activity?" "What is your other activity?" The 1981 census asked "Have you worked any time at all last year?" and then asked for "main activity" and "any other work".

Table 7. Sample activities included in four labour force definitions

		Labour Force Definition			
Activity		Paid LF (1)	Market LF (2)	New Standard LF (3)	Total LF (4)
1.	Non-agricultural work for wage or salary	yes	yes	yes	yes
2.	Agricultural work for wage or salary	yes	yes	yes	yes
3.	Family business, petty trading	no	yes	yes	yes
4.	Other self employment	no	yes	yes	yes
5.	Cooking meals for hired labourers	no	yes	yes	yes
6.	Weaving, sewing, other handcrafts	no	yes, if some products sold	yes	yes
7.	Farming for family	no	"	yes	yes
8.	Animal husbandry and kitchen gardening	no	"	yes	yes
9.	Processing crops for preservation or storage	no	"	yes	yes
10.	Gathering wild foods	no	"	yes	yes
11.	Gathering fuel or fodder	no	"	yes	yes
12.	Building and improving dwelling	no	no	yes	yes
13.	Maintaining dwelling (cleaning and repairs)	no	no	no	yes
14.	Collecting water for household use	no	no	no	yes
15.	Preparing meals, washing clothes, shopping, etc. for household	no	no	no	yes
16.	Caring for children and other family members	no	no	no	yes

Source: adapted from Anker, Khan and Gupta, 1987, p. 154.

When respondents are expected to answer questions such as these, they must interpret for themselves what is meant by the keywords or phrases such as "main activity" or "work for pay or profit". Complicating matters further, these keywords may not be meaningfully translated into local languages. Moreover, interviewers may "help" a hesitant respondent with inappropriate explanations or simply fill in the questionnaire based on his or her own assumptions.

There is evidence that respondents often fail to understand what is meant by particular keywords. A national sample survey in Kenya in 1974 revealed that activity rates for married women ages 20 to 49 varied from about 20 per cent to about 90 per cent, depending on whether the keyword used was "job" or "work" (Anker and Knowles, 1978). Apparently these Kenyan respondents considered that a "job" was paid wage or salary employment, whereas "work" was more broadly interpreted to include virtually all time-consuming activities required for the family's survival.

But in other settings the keyword "work" could also be misinterpreted as meaning "paid employment". The essence of the problem is that census-takers, male respondents, and even women themselves often view a wide range of activities other than purely domestic work as "housework" even if they provide some cash income (selling butter or a few surplus eggs, for example) and especially if they are primarily subsistence-oriented. In a study of women's economic activities in Chile, a researcher noted that "even if the wife herself works on the lands to which the family has access, she may or may not regard this as agricultural <u>work</u>. We were struck in interviewing women on large estates by the number of women who defined even planting and harvesting as <u>homemaking</u> rather than agricultural <u>work</u>" (Garrett, 1976:35; emphasis added).

How can such misunderstandings be minimised? One approach is to ask respondents whether or not they have engaged in any of an extensive list of specific activities, that is, to use an <u>activity schedule</u> tailored to local circumstances rather than the more general <u>keyword questionnaire</u>. This procedure has the advantage of specificity and thus greater accuracy, but has the disadvantages of length, more interview time, and thus more expensive data collection and analysis. As such, it is generally more suitable for sample surveys than for censuses, although the additional cost involved could be greatly reduced by using the activity schedule in combination with keyword questions. Appendix B describes a study in India comparing the results obtained from a simplified activity/time use schedule with those from a keyword questionnaire in a randomised experimental design.

Another approach is to arrange keyword or keyphrase questions in a logical sequence in which the meaning of each successive question is clarified with examples of the type of activity to be included. This technique is illustrated with a questionnaire in Appendix C. The questioning begins with a specific reference to activities that "resulted in income for you or your family" to identify the market-oriented labour force at once. It then proceeds to activities relating to the new standard labour force definition and the total labour force. Each question is followed with probes, which include the mention of specific activities, and with questions about the nature of the work performed and the time involved.

2. Primary and secondary occupations: dealing with multiple activities

Many census and survey questionnaires begin with a question such as "What is your main activity?" or "What is your primary occupation?" Whereas men will almost invariably state their occupation, women will often call themselves "housewives" even if they produce goods or services for the market. The issue here is not so much a misunderstanding of the concept, as discussed above, but how to elicit a fair representation of the time women spend in housework compared with their other productive activities. If the interviewer does not proceed with an additional question about secondary activities or occupations, the fact of women's employment may never be revealed. Even if the follow up question is asked, the results may not be used in the labour force tabulations. The exclusion of women reporting secondary but not primary economic activities undoubtedly contributed to the unusually low activity rates reported for women in the 1971 census of India. And according to the 1956 census of the Sudan the age-standardised labour force participation rate for women was less than 10 per cent when only primary occupations were included. But when women's secondary occupations were added, the female activity rate rose to 40 per cent (Durand, 1975:53). Similarly, in an experimental survey in India, activity rates rose from 3, 7, and 16 per cent in the paid, market, and internationally accepted labour forces, respectively, when based on responses to a question on "main activity," to 7, 18, and 41 per cent when a second question on "secondary activity" was also considered (Anker, Khan and Gupta, 1988).

The sequencing of questions recommended in the earlier discussion of the meaning of keywords (see Appendix C) is designed to minimise this type of bias. In a population census where space for additional questions is limited, the interviewer may stop asking questions as soon as some "economic" activity is identified. For example, most wage or salary employment would be identified in the first question. In labour force surveys, however, the interviewer should continue with additional questions even after obtaining a positive response in order to compile a more complete profile of each person's multiple economic activities. A person who earns money from wages or self-employment may also contribute to family income in other ways, e.g., through additional jobs, through subsistence production and processing, and through expenditure-saving labour within the household. Sample surveys that include more complex labour profiles such as these add immeasurably to our understanding of the diversity of economic activities among particular population subgroups according to age, ethnicity, and class. This is especially true of many Third World women who engage in a variety of labour force activities.

The neglect of multiple activities in data collection can lead to serious misperceptions of the true nature of rural (and urban) household incomes and labour supply. Because of this "disguised employment", planners may falsely assume that apparently surplus household labour can be mobilised for public works projects or other development schemes at little economic cost when in fact the diversion of labour will compete with other income sources and perhaps cause considerable hardship to low income households. Citing examples of such misperceptions and resulting hardships in two highland communities in Guatemala, Swetnam (1980) notes that the labour demands of subsistence agriculture, cash cropping, wage work, crafts, and trading among women and men in peasant household economies are delicately balanced, so that a change in one activity may disrupt a variety of other income sources. Planning and implementation of development policies must therefore reflect the realities of economic diversification. Adequate data are of course fundamental to this task.

3. The question of time: reference periods and hours worked

The issue of multiple economic activities is compounded by that of seasonal and other temporal variations in employment patterns for both women and men. Sample surveys in many developing countries have identified strong seasonal fluctuations in the number of days or hours people spend in agricultural and non-agricultural activities of different types as well as in housework. Although seasonality is most pronounced in agrarian settings, it also affects the patterns of many informal sector activities and even wage work.

Whereas the gainful worker approach to measuring economic activity inquires about a person's "usual" occupation, with a reference period such as past season or year, the more common labour force approach stresses current activity in a specified brief period such as the day or week preceding the interview. The ILO has recommended in the past that the time-reference period not be longer than one week except "where it is considered that classification on the basis of current activity over this brief time period does not reflect year-round activities, particularly where there is a highly seasonal pattern of employment" (ILO, 1976).

A short reference period is likely to exclude many women, however, particularly where their economic activities are more seasonal than men's. In Peru, for example, the 1940 census counted women as only 14 per cent of the agricultural labour force when the question was based on "present" occupation in a specified week but as 31 per cent when the question was based on "usual" occupation (Durand, 1975:241). Similarly, according to the 1971 census of Indonesia, women comprised 32 per cent of the agricultural labour force when the question referred to employment during the "previous week" (which was a slack season) as against 41 per cent when the question referred to the "last cropping season" (World Bank, 1980:23-4).

Each of these figures provides valuable information for planners: the usual labour force captures regular and seasonal activities and the current labour force captures the particulars of a specified short period. Our feeling is that questions proposed above should be asked both for the preceding week and for the preceding season or year. If only one reference period is used, the latter is preferable. Many persons earn income irregularly, e.g., working as an agricultural labourer or on a family farm or preparing meals for workers only in periods of peak demand; or husking wheat or rice only at the end of the growing season; or doing petty trading or sewing on an irregular basis.

The more difficult issue is what criterion to adopt for the minimum number of hours required for inclusion in the economically active population. Again, this issue is confounded by the diversity and irregularity of activity profiles for most workers, especially among the poorest sectors of the population and in subsistence agriculture.

As noted earlier, the conventional practice based on internationally accepted definitions of 1954 and 1966 has been to require unpaid family helpers to work at least one-third of the "normal" working time (however defined, but typically taken to be 10 or 15 hours per week) during the reference period in order to be counted as employed. For those who generate cash income as well as those said to be self-employed, however, one hour during the preceding week was typically used.

This differential treatment of persons earning wage or salary income and self-employed persons making productive contributions to family income, on the one hand, and of unpaid family workers on the other hand, incorporated a strong gender bias because women were very often considered to be unpaid family workers. For this reason, the 1982 International Conference of Labour Statisticians (ICLS) eliminated the distinction between self-employed and unpaid family workers as far as the minimum time criterion is concerned. It substituted the criterion of making "an important contribution" to household consumption for those who work without pay in a family farm or other family enterprise. Gender bias was perpetuated because this criterion is not required of those who earn money, no matter how little. Moreover, as the new criterion is probably impossible to operationalise, the most common solution has been to estimate the "importance" of a contribution by the old criterion of number of hours worked. But again, should paid and unpaid workers be treated differently? If so, then the selective underenumeration of women (and children) will be perpetuated, and their total contributions to the household economy and to national development will continue to be devalued. If not, then the minimum number of hours required for inclusion in the labour force should be the same for all categories of workers.

Unpublished data from a study in Egypt of approximately 1,000 rural adult women illustrates how sensitive female labour force estimates are to the time criteria used. Minimum requirements were set at "any time at all", one hour, 4 hours, 7 hours, 10 hours, and 15 hours. As indicated in Table 8, almost no women who were eligible for inclusion in the paid labour force, the market labour force, or the new standard labour force were excluded on the grounds of having worked less than one hour in the previous week. This finding suggests that the one-hour minimum time requirement in the reference week is meaningless; it is just too low to eliminate many women from the labour force. Increasing the minimum time required to 15 hours in the reference week causes the estimated activity rates to decrease from 12.0 to 9.3 per cent in the paid labour force, from 37.1 to 23.7 per cent in the market labour force, and from 79.8 to 42.3 per cent in the new standard labour force.

In sum, the ways in which concepts are defined and the ways in which questions are asked about labour force activity are likely to make little difference in the resulting counts of the male labour force for most countries and population subgroups. But they are likely to make a great difference in the enumeration of the female labour force, and thus in estimates of the total. Because there is great variation from country to country and even within countries in the meanings of words, in the range of typical activities, and in the "normal" use of time, we strongly recommend that different definitions and methods of data collection be tested in the field in sample surveys prior to large-scale censuses or surveys. In this way the results of contrasting approaches can be compared systematically with an experimental research design (see Appendix B). It is important to stress also that the definitions and procedures to be used depend on the purposes of the data. What is appropriate for one set of planning tasks may be inappropriate for another. Thinking through in the initial planning stages exactly how the data will be used will help to structure the definitions, collection, and analysis.

Table 8. Estimated female labour force activity rates in rural Egypt
based on different minimum time requirements for past week reference period

Labour force definition	Activity rate with minimum time of					
	any time (1)	one hour (2)	four hours (3)	seven hours (4)	ten hours (5)	fifteen hours (6)
Paid LF	12.0	11.9	11.4	11.0	10.7	9.3
Market LF	37.1	37.0	34.6	33.4	29.2	23.7
New Standard LF	79.8	79.0	70.8	66.8	54.3	42.3

Source: Anker and Anker, forthcoming, based on data from ILO/CAPMAS methods test, Oct.-Nov. 1983 survey. Sample size is approximately 1, 024.

IV. BEYOND LABOUR FORCE PARTICIPATION: ASSESSING OTHER ASPECTS OF WOMEN'S ECONOMIC CONTRIBUTIONS

The accurate measurement of women's labour force participation as reviewed above is critical to development planning. But labour force participation is only one dimension of economic activity: it gives little hint of time use, the productivity of labour, returns to labour, or the importance of women's labour and earnings to the household and to the national economy. In this section we review some methodological and analytical issues relating to each of these additional dimensions of economic activity. Each has relevance to planners, in different ways.

A. The Use of Time

Whereas labour force censuses and surveys measure the <u>stock</u> of workers at one point in time, most time-use surveys attempt to measure the <u>flow</u> of labour throughout the day, the week, the season, and the year. The typical time-use survey collects information from direct observation or from respondents' recall on the time spent during the day on a variety of activities for all household members above a certain age. The purpose is to obtain statistical profiles of how household members allocate their time. Such data permit analysis of differences in time-use patterns according to individual and household characteristics such as the person's age, sex, and relationship to other household members, and the household's size, age-sex composition, and ethnic, caste, and class status. Daily, weekly, and seasonal variations in time use can also be identified, as well as variations based on environmental, economic and cultural conditions, on relationship to employers, control over resources, and other factors of interest.

Time-use surveys covering the full range of possible activities usually divide total waking hours into aggregated activity categories, each of which in turn is composed of a detailed set of activities. The three most commonly used general activity categories are: <u>economic activities</u> (which include market work, market-oriented production, subsistence-based economic production); <u>housework and child care</u> (which include domestic work, household maintenance and child care); and <u>non-work</u> (which includes leisure, recreation, eating, resting, personal maintenance, visiting). Studies occasionally specify separately other categories such as schooling and other training, or participation in community projects or extended economic activities such as food processing and fuel gathering.

Within the broad category of economic activities, time may be classified by type of work (e.g., crop cultivation, animal husbandry, professional and technical work, crafts, business and trade, domestic work for pay, etc.); by mode of payment (e.g., unpaid work for home consumption, production for sale or trade in a family enterprise, work for wages, exchange labour); or by other criteria of interest such as location (e.g., at or near home, away from home in village or neighborhood, outside of village) and the presence or absence of co-workers, supervisors, or dependents (e.g., young children).

A detailed survey of time use of all household members can form the basis for allocating persons to the four labour force categories proposed in Section III. But it provides much additional information as well. It identifies patterns of over- and underemployment, either seasonal or year round, for specific household members. Moreoever, just as one can calculate from censuses the female share of the total labour force according to occupation or employment status, one can calculate from time-use surveys the female share of total labour hours spent by household members on specified productive activities. In this sense, time is used as a direct measure of economic contributions. Time-use profiles can also be devised for each respondent showing the per centage of total waking hours he or she devotes to each activity. The aggregated profiles can then be classified by age, sex, and other variables of interest such as social class, place of work, and relationship to employer. The problems of data collection and analysis are complex, however, and the interpretation of results can pose a challenge.

1. Methodological problems of collecting time-use data

Information about how people spend their time is notoriously difficult to collect for a number of reasons. These include respondents' lack of awareness of time on the clock, inevitable trouble with estimation and recall, deciding when one activity ends and another begins, dealing with the simultaneous performance of two or more activities, including or excluding travel time, relying on "proxies" to report on what other family members are doing, and so on. As a result, it is often difficult to compare results from different time-use surveys. For example, some surveys record information on time spent in all activities, including those performed simultaneously (e.g., both cooking and child-care when done at the same time); others do not allow for the separate recording of simultaneous activities and so record only the time spent on one activity in each time period, which is considered to be the primary activity. In the latter type of time-use survey, the total time taken for all activities cannot exceed 24 hours per day and so activities that are usually performed simultaneously with other tasks (e.g., child-care) would be underreported as compared with the former survey format.

The three most common methods of data collection -- direct observation, interviews using recall, and respondent record-keeping -- result in different levels of accuracy as well as

three months), respondents were asked how frequently they performed the task: "throughout the season", "most of the time", "some of the time", or "rarely or occasionally". These rough categories were then translated into estimates of numbers of hours and days for the data analysis (Anker, Khan and Gupta, 1987:155). Although some detail is inevitably lost, the approximations were felt to be reasonably accurate and to be useful for describing labour profiles for individual respondents and thus for the entire sample. This approach could also be used to contrast current activities (e.g., previous day or week) with usual activities (previous season or year). Thus it is possible to gain some idea of fluctuations in activity patterns -- of possible labour bottlenecks or surpluses impeding productivity, for example -- even from a single survey.

2. Interpreting time-use data: illustrations from Asia

Information collected from a survey of time use by household members in a village of Nepal is presented for selected age groups in Table 9. Hours per person per day spent in various work activities are averaged here in a way that obscures seasonal, weekly and daily variations (although these could be indicated in a different tabulation) but highlights typical activity contrasts by age and gender.

What major conclusions can be drawn from Table 9? First, females in this sample in all three age groups worked about two hours longer during the day on average in all work activities combined than males did. The average work-day for adult women was about 12 to 13 hours, for adult men about 10 hours. Girls aged 12 to 14 averaged almost the same number of total work hours per day as did adult men. Second, girls aged 12 to 14 spent more time than boys the same age in all so-called directly productive activities, while adult women spent only slightly less time (about one-half hour less per day) than men the same age. For both sexes, hours spent on what the researchers called directly productive work peaked at ages 20 to 29. Certain productive activities took more female than male hours: agricultural work on the household's own land, for example, and agricultural wage labour. Note, too, the large amount of time spent by both females and males (especially at younger ages) tending animals. Third, females spent about twice the number of hours per day on household work than did males in each age group, with total hours peaking for both sexes at ages 40 to 49. Although these data are drawn from a single village, they offer important information to planners of village-based projects on the extensive work commitments of both women and men. These are useful for designing training and credit programmes (for example, farm credit for women as well as men) or for providing other inputs to raise productivity and incomes, among other purposes. Further analysis could take into account such factors as the total number of people in the household, age of youngest child, amount of land held, seasonal differences in work patterns, and the household's access to other production assets.

Table 9. Average hours per person per day in work activities by sex in a Nepalese village, selected age groups, 1972-73

| Activity | Ages 12-14 | | Ages 20-29 | | Ages 40-49 | |
	Males (1)	Females (2)	Males (3)	Females (4)	Males (5)	Females (6)
1. Wage labour (nonagricultural)	0.2	0.0	0.5	0.1	0.6	0.0
2. Wage labour (agricultural)	0.1	1.2	2.1	1.8	1.1	1.9
3. Production of articles for sale	0.1	0.4	0.7	0.4	0.8	0.2
4. Handicrafts	0.1	0.0	0.3	0.1	0.5	0.2
5. Agricultural work (own land)	1.3	1.5	2.8	3.3	2.8	3.0
6. Animal care	3.7	3.5	2.0	2.5	2.1	1.8
7. Reciprocal labour exchange, community work	0.0	0.0	0.4	0.2	0.0	0.0
Total directly productive work (1-7)	5.5	6.6	8.8	8.4	7.9	7.1
8. Firewood collection	0.2	0.2	0.3	0.2	0.3	0.1
9. Other household maintenance work	0.5	1.0	0.6	1.0	0.9	1.1
10. Household food preparation	0.9	1.5	0.7	1.8	1.0	3.1
11. Child care	0.2	0.6	0.0	0.7	0.3	1.3
Total household maintenance (8-11)	1.8	3.3	1.6	3.7	2.5	5.6
Total all work (1-11)	7.3	9.9	10.4	12.1	10.4	12.7
(Number of persons)	(51)	(25)	(20)	(28)	(33)	(34)

Source: Adapted from Nag, White, and Peet, 1980, pp. 254-5.

incurring different costs in terms of time, effort, and expense (Dixon-Mueller, 1985:36-42). In each case, deciding on the appropriate number and classification of <u>activity categories</u> is difficult. On the one hand, one wants to include sufficiently detailed break downs so that questions of the desired specificity can be answered. On the other hand, the complexities of data collection, processing and analysis with many activities where repeated time-use readings are taken throughout the year can quickly become overwhelming.

For all three methods, <u>observers and interviewers</u> need to be highly trained in eliciting reliable measures of time use and in sorting out one activity from another in a consistent and comparable way. Interviewer or observer bias can easily confound the responses. <u>Sampling</u> is also a key issue in each method, not only of individuals or households but also of reference periods (Connell and Lipton, 1977; Casely and Lury, 1980). The number of reference periods should be selected so as to minimise chance variation and at the same time to capture the daily, weekly, or seasonal activity cycles of most interest. This might for example imply an interview each month for one year using a one day reference period, or interviews in each of four seasons using a one week reference period, or some other combination. For all of these reasons, time-use surveys are difficult and expensive to conduct. Almost always restricted to specific locales with relatively small samples, they are rarely generalisable to national populations.

Simplified time-use surveys can be feasible for national samples, however, if one is willing to accept the loss of repeated interviews using short-term recall and rely on a single interview with both short-term and long-term recall. This would include the use of an <u>activity-specific recall</u> type of interview which begins with a pre-set list of activities and asks the respondent to indicate if he or she has done any of these activities and, if so, to recall the approximate time spent on each during the preceding day, week, month, or year, depending on the cycle of the activity in question. Questions may be framed in terms of "hours in previous day", "days last week", and "hours per day (when done)". The longer is the reference period, the more difficult it is for respondents to estimate the amount of time spent in each activity. An Indonesian study concluded that estimates of total labour time based on a one-month reference period averaged about 60 to 70 per cent of those based on a one-day reference period, with no consistent pattern of differences in under-reporting by gender or social class (Wigna <u>et al</u>, 1980:7).

A simplified activity/time questionnaire used in the Uttar Pradesh survey mentioned above offers a feasible alternative to the requirement that respondents estimate the actual number of hours (or fractions of hours) they spend on each activity. Respondents were asked whether they had performed during the past year any of 15 productive tasks. Those who said yes were asked approximately how much time they spent on each activity during the days when it was done: "a small amount of time", "less than half the working day", "about half", "more than half", or "a full day". For an estimate of total time spent during the past cropping season (about

Table 10 presents similar data for a Javanese village in which average hours per month contributed by female and male household members to four income-earning activities and to housework are identified by class (three categories of landowning status) and by season (peak and slack agricultural months). These figures reveal very interesting patterns of economic activity.

First, considering all work activities combined, women's contribution grows in both absolute terms (total hours, column 9) and relative to men's (per centage of total hours, column 10) as one moves "downward" in social class from the large landowners to the landless. This is true of both peak and slack months. Depending on landowning status, women contributed from 44 to 49 per cent of total work hours in the peak month and from 38 to 51 per cent in the slack month.

Second, women's contribution to total income-earning activities (columns 5 and 6) was also higher in absolute and relative terms among the landless than among landowners. For both seasons, women contributed approximately 20 per cent of total household hours spent on income-generating work among large landowners, approximately 30 per cent among small landowners, and approximately 40 per cent among the landless. Among the four income-earning activities it is clear that access to production resources is a crucial determinant of both male and female time-use patterns. In general, the number of hours women and men spent on production on their own land and on trading dropped markedly from landowners to the landless, while hours spent on wage labour and on searching activities (collecting fuel, wild foods, etc. for sale) rose -- especially in the slack month.

Third, the number of hours women spent on housework (column 7) also drops from large landowners to the landless, as one would expect, for both seasons. But men contributed more hours to housework during the slack season, especially among the large landowners. As a consequence, whereas the female share of household time ranges from 92 to 96 per cent in the peak month, it ranges from 82 to 90 per cent in the slack month.

Other findings of relevance to planners could be extracted from the table. What is important here is the realisation that women's and men's labour contributions to income generation and household maintenance respond differently to fluctuations in seasonal labour demand and to class-based conditions such as landowning status (a surrogate measure of other assets as well). The data also underscore a more general set of conclusions drawn from research throughout the Third World: (1) the economic performance of households in the lowest income brackets is directly related to the economic activity of women in these households; (2) the importance of women's productive role increases with poverty but the extent of their reproductive functions does not diminish, resulting in a dual burden for poor women; and (3) a

Table 10. Average labour hours per month per household by sex and household's landowning status for peak and slack agricultural months in a Javanese village, 1972-73

Landowning status and season	Sex	Hours per month per household				Income earning activities		Housework activities		All work activities	
		Own production (1)	Trading (2)	Wage labour (3)	Searching activities (4)	Total hours (5)	% of total (6)	Total hours (7)	% of total (8)	Total hours (9)	% of total (10)
Peak Month											
Large landowners	Female	18.1	29.9	42.7	5.2	95.9	23.6	153.1	95.8	249.0	44.1
	Male	271.0	15.0	22.0	1.6	309.5	76.4	6.7	4.2	316.2	55.9
Small landowners	Female	10.5	36.5	92.9	32.3	171.1	32.8	116.3	93.3	287.4	44.5
	Male	103.8	9.0	186.3	51.1	350.1	67.2	8.4	6.7	358.5	55.5
Landless	Female	2.3	12.9	153.5	26.5	195.1	40.1	94.9	92.0	290.0	49.2
	Male	17.9	0	237.1	36.2	291.2	59.9	8.2	8.0	299.4	50.8
Slack Month											
Large landowners	Female	25.6	25.8	8.6	16.1	76.1	19.0	136.7	82.0	212.8	37.6
	Male	290.0	13.6	15.0	4.8	323.4	81.0	30.0	18.0	353.4	62.4
Small landowners	Female	5.3	55.4	41.4	20.3	122.4	27.5	113.8	90.2	236.2	41.4
	Male	81.7	5.3	123.5	111.6	322.2	72.5	12.4	9.8	334.6	58.6
Landless	Female	5.9	8.6	138.4	42.6	195.5	41.9	97.7	90.5	293.2	51.1
	Male	21.6	0	104.6	144.5	270.7	58.1	10.2	9.5	280.9	48.9

Note: Figures are based on all household members aged six years or more in a stratified random sample of 86 households.

Source: Hart, 1980, p. 204.

major goal of development policy should be to increase the productivity and income of women in the lowest income households (Buvinic, 1983:16).

Many additional examples of interesting time-use presentations could be cited (see, e.g., Dixon-Mueller 1985:43-56; Goldschmidt-Clermont 1987a:14-22). Among these are illustrations of surveys used to obtain precise measures of change in patterns of labour allocation for women and men according to task and crop resulting from specific agricultural interventions. Time-use data are particularly useful in pinpointing the differential impact of introducing new crops and new technologies on male and female labour requirements, and in identifying critical labour bottlenecks. Typical among these are the additional work burdens placed on women for harvesting, processing and storing high-yield varieties of grains. The data can also identify areas of low productivity where training or improved technologies could reduce the amount of time spent on repetitive and time-consuming tasks yielding low returns -- tasks in which female (and child) labour is most likely to be concentrated. The data can also indicate to planners the extent to which men and women are underemployed and so in need of, and available for, new development activities.

What implications do time-use data have for labour, population and development planning? How does the availability of time-use data -- as opposed to the usual labour force data -- affect planning differently? By providing a detailed and reasonably accurate description of labour time classified by gender, social class, location, etc., time-use surveys provide development planners with the basic information required for deciding on appropriate policies. For example, planners need to know what type of persons or households (e.g., men or women, adults or children, rich or poor, landed or landless) are most in need of employment, extension services, training, credit, or marketing assistance. Planners also need to know who is in a position to take advantage of (or be adversely affected by) a new project such as a dam, factory, road, or employment scheme. Rather than portraying women as non-workers or grossly underemployed workers, as often occurs when conclusions are drawn from labour force surveys, time-use surveys present a complete picture that stresses the heavy work burden of women. This, in turn, implies that governments interested in increasing women's outputs and productivity in so-called "economic" activities need to consider ways of reducing the long hours and low productivity of domestic activities such as food processing, cooking and water-fetching. It also implies that governments interested in expanding the employment of women away from home should be aware of the need for providing sufficiently high wages or incomes to women so as to compensate them and their families for the value of the domestic work which has to be foregone.

B. Sex Differences in Labour Productivity

The numbers of hours or days spent on an activity is a simple measure of labour inputs, and thus of women's contribution to the total work effort. But it conveys little about the productivity of labour, defined as the output of goods or services per person-hour of labour invested. Labour productivity depends on the amount of human energy and skill applied to the task at hand (i.e., on labour inputs; on non-labour inputs such as mechanical equipment, animal power, improved seeds and fertilisers, technology employed, etc.; and on the management efficiency with which the two are combined (i.e, how labour is organised and how efficiently capital is used) (Standing 1977).

Identifying economic activities of particularly low productivity is an important task for planners because it pinpoints areas of sub-optimal use of human and other resources. Time-consuming tasks with low output result in low economic returns and thus perpetuate the cycle of poverty. In many cases, productivity can be improved significantly with carefully designed inputs of training, capital in the form of credit, and improved technology, among other investments. This is especially true in agriculture and in the urban informal sector.

The measurement of gender differences in labour productivity is a complicated matter. Yet it is crucial to understanding the extent to which women as a group are working under disadvantaged conditions. In turn, it is crucial to understanding inequities inherent in the differential social and economic returns to male and female labour.

1. Labour inputs affecting productivity

People work at different intensities and efficiencies, depending on their physical strength, dexterity, and endurance; on their general knowledge and special skills; and on their interest and motivation, among other factors. Sex differences in labour productivity will be affected by all of these characteristics, each of which in turn depends on a number of background factors.

Physical strength, dexterity, and endurance, for example, will depend in part on nutritional levels of workers, on the quantity and quality of health care, and on the availability of rest and leisure. In many developing countries, girls and women (especially those among the poorest classes) are especially disadvantaged in comparison with boys and men in access to these resources. In some countries, indicators of sex differences are available at the national level for mortality by cause at each age, for the prevalence of certain illnesses, for per capita consumption of calories and/or animal protein, and for visits to hospitals and health practitioners, among other indicators. Time-use surveys such as the Nepal study cited above can identify patterns of overwork among women who -- almost everywhere -- are found to have significantly fewer hours of rest and leisure than men.

Girls and women tend to be similarly disadvantaged in the formal acquisition of general knowledge and special skills that could improve their labour productivity and returns. National-level indicators of sex differentials in access to formal schooling, for example, include the ratios of females to males who are literate, who are enrolled in primary, secondary, and tertiary schooling, who have completed each level of schooling, who specialise in each academic discipline (e.g., science, engineering), and who are enrolled in vocational training courses of various types. These ratios identify the areas in which females are over- and underrepresented in proportion to their numbers in the population. The data are useful for planners in revealing how early patterns of sex segregation begin to appear at the national level in the formal schooling system (e.g., in the enrollment rates of young children) and the particular direction they take. Data can also be collected from employee surveys on their access to specific job-related training. A 1981 survey in Cyprus, for example, found that higher percentages of male than female employees had received on-the-job training or out-of-firm training within each age group and occupational category (House, 1986:145). These data point to clear inequities of direct policy relevance because they affect worker performance and efficiency.

Labour productivity also depends on the worker's motivation and interest, which in turn depend on factors such as the nature and urgency of the task (its repetitiveness, importance, etc.), on the nature and degree of positive and negative sanctions governing task performance, and on labour turnover and the commitment of employers to a stable labour force. The segregation of women into occupations or activities of higher repetitiveness and lower returns is bound to affect overall labour productivity. The higher are the social and economic returns to labour, the higher will be the worker's motivation. In turn, negative sanctions such as threats of dismissal for poor performance or extreme economic pressures on the worker which are intended to increase labour productivity in the short run may have the opposite effect over the long run. The segregation of women into occupations with high labour turnover and little opportunity for on-the-job experience or promotion also affects total labour productivity.

2. Non-labour inputs affecting productivity

Worker productivity also depends on access to non-labour inputs such as land, capital in the form of credit or personal assets, tools and other labour-saving equipment, draft animals, transportation, technical assistance, and other assets or services such as membership in co-operatives. Each of these can be measured in sample surveys. Table 11, for example, illustrates the average value of farm assets for male-headed and female-headed households in rural Botswana in 1974-75. The value of cattle, small stock, land, and equipment of female-headed

Table 11. Mean value of assets (in rands) for male-headed and female-headed households, rural Botswana, 1974-75

| Assets | Household Composition[a] | | | | |
	MH-MP (1)	MH-NMP (2)	FH-MP (3)	FH-NMP (4)	Total (5)
Value of cattle					
Per household	1,322	1,749	903	439	1,066
Per person	180	274	119	85	159
Per adult equivalent	261	411	171	138	237
Value of small stock					
Per household	145	218	131	72	129
Per person	20	34	17	14	19
Per adult equivalent	29	51	25	23	29
Value of land acreage					
Per household	14	14	12	6	11
Per person	2	2	2	1	2
Per adult equivalent	3	3	2	2	3
Value of equipment					
Per household	334	201	182	94	237
Per person	45	31	24	18	35
Per adult equivalent	66	47	34	30	53
Number of households	(452)	(77)	(131)	(277)	(957) [b]
Percentage of households	49	8	13	28	100

Notes:

a   MH-MP   : Recognised male head, working age male present (age 20-64).
     MH-NMP   : Recognised male head, no working age male present.
     FH-MP   : Recognised female head, working age male present.
     FH-NMP   : Recognised female head, no working age male present.

b   Includes 20 households (2 per cent of total) with head unidentified.

Source: Kossoudji and Mueller, 1981, p. 44.

households with no adult male present (column 4) was only about one-third to one-half that of male-headed households (columns 1 and 2) on a per household, per person, and per adult basis. Female-headed households with a working age male present (column 3) occupied an intermediate position. About four in ten households in this survey were headed by women.

Because women generally have less access to non-labour inputs than men, even where they are performing the same tasks, it is difficult to obtain "pure" measures of sex differences in labour productivity that are not confounded by the effects of non-labour inputs. In agriculture, for example, women often work by hand while men appropriate the more advanced technology -- the chemical fertilisers spread by machine rather than the organic ones spread by hand tools, or the machine rather than the manual threshers. Moreoever, a simple substitution of tools may change the sex-typing of a task and widen the productivity gap where men take over the new techniques and leave women to the hand operations.

In agricultural research, the productivity of workers -- that is, output per person-hour -- is frequently expressed in terms of "adult male equivalents". Thus, the productivity of an adult female worker may be assumed to be only 60 or 75 per cent as great as that of an adult male, and that of workers from 10 to 14 to be only 30 or 50 per cent of an adult male (see Dixon-Mueller 1985:64-65 for other examples).

These estimates of adult male equivalent workers suffer from several problems. First, they are almost never based on measures of actual output. Rather, they are based on ad hoc assumptions, or, in some cases, on hourly wage differences that reflect the confounding influences of labour market discrimination. Second, they obscure important variations among tasks or activities, e.g., between those in which women specialise (but men perform occasionally) and vice versa. Third, they almost always confound the effects of labour inputs and non-labour inputs on total productivity. Direct comparisons of male and female workers engaged in the same tasks with the same equipment are rare. In an early Korean farm study the relative efficiency of men, women, and boys aged 12 to 18 was measured according to the average area ploughed, transplanted, weeded, and harvested in one hour for paddy and other crops. Women in this comparison averaged about half the efficiency of men on most tasks and about the same as teenage boys. In contrast, a more recent Indian Government study found women to be about three times as efficient as men when tested on two types of potato-digging equipment, as measured by average amount picked per minute (cited in Dixon-Mueller, 1985:62-64).

It is possible to disentangle the effects of labour and non-labour inputs on total productivity by means of multivariate analysis. In a study in western Kenya, for example, the output of maize per acre from female-managed farms (almost 40 per cent of all farms) was only slightly lower on average than that of male-managed farms (but with higher variation) despite women's significantly lower use of chemical fertilisers, hybrid plants, insecticides, and extension services and loans (Moock, 1976:832). Indeed, female-headed farms averaged lower on 13 of 15 measures of farm inputs. Although women farmers applied marginally higher labour inputs in hours per acre and a slightly higher proportion of women interplanted maize with legumes, the results of a regression analysis indicated that "these women were more technically efficient maize farmers than the men" in achieving significantly higher outputs at mean levels of input use. Labour efficiency in the production of maize -- the main subsistence crop in Kenya -- was isolated here through statistical techniques rather than through controlled observations.

The results of the Kenyan study should not be taken as evidence that women's restricted access to non-labour inputs does not have a negative impact on female labour productivity, however (e.g., see Staudt, 1985 for another Kenyan example). Rather, inequities in access to the resources mentioned above, by affecting both labour and non-labour inputs, serve as a major constraint on the effective utilisation of women's energies and skills in almost every setting. Where women succeed in achieving a high level of productivity, it is usually despite the obstacles that they face in comparison with their male counterparts, rather than because of special advantages they may have. These disadvantages in gaining access to nonlabour inputs such as credit, new technologies, and training cause the total output of the economy to be lower than it could be. In addition, misallocation of resources of this type has a disproportionately larger impact on poorer households, where returns from women's labour are crucial for survival. This is true both in female-headed households, where women are the sole or main provider, as well as in poor male-headed or jointly-headed households where the efforts of both men and women are required to meet the family's basic human needs.

C. Measuring the Returns to Labour: Wages and Other Income

Returns to labour, as defined here, refer to the benefits accruing to the worker from his or her efforts. These include wages or income earned from self-employment; income flowing to the household from joint activities in a household enterprise; and expenditures foregone by the individual or the household as a result of the worker's efforts, e.g, in subsistence production.

Returns to labour are often social as well, although these are not discussed in detail here. Suffice it to say that many activities carry high prestige value; many convey a strong sense of personal pride and satisfaction to the person performing them; and many involve considerable social interaction that workers may enjoy. The extent to which certain activities are socially recognised and rewarded -- that is, are "status-enhancing" rather than "status-degrading" -- forms an important element of the labour process that also differentiates male and female workers within specific caste and class contexts. Critics of conventional economic and labour statistics have noted that much of the underreporting of the amount and value of women's work derives from precisely those social attitudes that tend to place a higher value on what men do than what women do. When these attitudes become internalised, women become active agents in undervaluing and underestimating their own contributions to the household and national economies.

1. Sex differences in wages

Evidence from national surveys reveals pervasive wage differences between male and female workers in every country. A survey of agricultural wage rates paid to male and female workers in six states of India, for example, found that women's rates averaged about 80 per cent of men's rates at the minimum scales for sowers, weeders, and reapers, and 73 per cent at the maximum scales. The ratio of female to male rates was slightly higher on average for plantation workers in tea, coffee, and rubber (79 per cent) than for other agricultural labourers (75 per cent) (see Dixon-Mueller 1985:72).

Table 12 reports ratios of female to male earnings (wage rates) in manufacturing industries for 14 developing countries for years between 1972 and 1985, as listed in the ILO **Year Book of Labour Statistics.** With an overall average of 67 per cent, female wage rates ranged from 46 per cent of male rates in the Republic of Korea and 52 per cent in Cyprus to 83 per cent in El Salvador and 90 per cent in Burma. Figures for some countries fluctuate wildly from year to year, however, and are thus not reliable for establishing firm levels or trends. Moreoever, country estimates are not directly comparable with one another because of differences in sampling techniques and measurement, among other factors.

Despite these qualifications, the figures in Table 12 are typical of the marked disparities in wages between women and men in developing countries (as well as in more industrialised nations). Wage gaps vary substantially according to the supply of and demand for male and female workers in different economic sectors. The ratio of female to male wages for farm labourers, for instance, tends to rise during seasons of peak demand and drop in the slack months. Sex differentials in wage rates also vary according to governmental policies and the practices of private employers. Indeed, societal, employer, and governmental norms and biases about the "rightful place" of males and females in the economy and in the labour force greatly constrain the opportunities open to women.

Space does not permit a detailed discussion of the basis of differential wage rates and other economic benefits for male and female workers (see Anker and Hein 1986 for a general overview of the situation and seven detailed country case studies). Among the many contributing factors that must be disentangled are the propensity for women to be more concentrated than

Table 12. Female earnings as per centage of male earnings in manufacturing industries, selected countries[a], 1972-85

Region and country	1972	1973	1974	1975	1976	1977	1978	1979	1980	1981	1982	1983	1984	1985
Sub-Saharan Africa														
Kenya	–	–	–	66	77	56	54	70	62	58	76	78	77	–
Swaziland	–	–	–	–	66	78	71	83	81	82	81	61	–	–
Tanzania	79	79	82	71	79	88	82	81	78	78	–	–	–	–
North Africa, Middle East														
Cyprus	68	65	–	47	49	50	48	50	50	54	56	55	55	56
Egypt	–	–	63	68	75	63	92	–	–	–	–	–	–	–
Jordan	–	–	–	–	–	–	54	60	58	64	60	63	–	–
Syria	55	59	65	70	65	69	–	–	–	–	–	–	–	–
South, Southeast, East Asia														
Burma	94	89	85	88	82	103	87	89	86	89	90	92	–	–
Hong Kong	–	–	–	–	–	–	–	–	–	–	78	79	81	79
Rep. Korea	–	–	–	47	49	45	44	44	45	45	45	46	47	47
Singapore	–	–	–	–	–	–	–	–	62	62	63	64	65	63
Sri Lanka	–	–	–	–	–	–	–	–	75	78	81	73	67	70
Central America, Caribbean														
El Salvador	79	82	83	90	86	81	82	79	81	86	–	–	–	–
Netherlands Antilles	–	–	–	–	–	–	–	–	51	66	64	67	68	–

a   All developing countries with wages reported by sex in source.

Source: ILO, **Year Book of Labour Statistics**, 1986, Table 17a; Anker and Hein, 1986, p. 104.

men in lower-skilled and lower-productivity occupations or tasks (for example, in service occupations and -- within the manufacturing industries -- in lower-paying occupations); to have more job interruptions due to marriage and child-bearing and thus fewer average years of experience; to have less formal schooling or specialised training; and to work fewer hours in the day, week, season, or year.

Unfortunately, simple bivariate analyses of the relationship between average monthly earnings of women and men and, say, years of schooling or average hours worked is insufficient to identify the separate and independent effects of each factor. Multivariate analyses which can be used for this purpose invariably identify a large gender gap in earnings after controlling simultaneously for a wide range of contributing factors. They indicate substantial wage discrimination based on gender. Indeed, in many cases minimum wage rates set by governments or private employers are lower for women than men. Most of the other contributing factors mentioned above also signify strong patterns of selective socialisation of females into particular occupational roles in addition to active sex discrimination in education and employment.

Data on women's wage rates and earnings by age are crucial for a number of analytical purposes (Mueller, 1983:277-8). First, it is important to distinguish among women who earn little because they are not engaged in full time work, and those who earn little because of low wage rates (or both). Second, economists consider the wage rate an important factor affecting household decisions regarding who will seek employment and the amount of time worked. They are likely to have a strong influence on migration decisions, for example, for females (in most settings) as well as males. The wage rates obtainable by young girls (and boys) determine the opportunity cost of time spent in school. In addition, wage rates paid to women of reproductive age, considered jointly with the probability of finding employment, represent an opportunity cost of time spent on housework and child care. Thus they are useful for studies of the economic aspects of fertility decisions, among other purposes.

2. Self-employment: agriculture and the urban informal sector

The tendency for women working as own-account or unpaid family workers to have more limited access to production resources such as capital, equipment, and transportation to markets inevitably lowers the returns to their labour. This is true of both agricultural and non-agricultural sectors.

(a) Within agriculture, women are enumerated in population censuses as own-account or self-employed workers if they produce and sell crops or animals on their "own account" or (more rarely) hire other workers to do so. Women (or men) are enumerated as unpaid family workers if they work in a family enterprise under the "direction" of an own-account worker. The

58

boundary line between self-employment and unpaid family labour is obviously difficult to draw. Countries differ in their enumeration practices, although there is a distinct tendency for gender bias as women are much more likely than men to be considered unpaid family workers. An examination of census data from 58 developing countries with classifications by employment status finds that approximately 40 per cent of the female agricultural labour force in sub-Saharan Africa are enumerated as self-employed. This figure compares with about 30 per cent in Central and South America and the Caribbean, about 20 per cent in Asia, and about 15 per cent in North Africa and the Middle East. On average, however, women are underrepresented among the self-employed relative to their enumerated share of the total farm labour force (a 12 per cent share in self-employment compared with a 22 per cent share in unpaid family labour for 58 developing countries).

Where women sell at least some of their farm produce and are thus enumerated (theoretically) as own-account workers, the economic returns to their labour can be measured by subtracting from their earnings the value of any wages paid in cash or kind and of non-labour inputs such as seeds and fertilisers, land and equipment, and transport and storage. The value of inputs used for both market-oriented and subsistence-oriented production would have to be apportioned according to the per centage of total output that is sold. Complications arise where other family members have contributed unpaid labour, however, which makes the calculation of separate returns for male and female own-account workers in family farms a tricky business. Comparisons of economic returns to male- and female-headed farm households are more straightforward.

The policy relevant question here is how the returns to women's self-employment in agriculture could be raised in order to enable rural households to meet more effectively their basic human needs. In sub-Saharan Africa, for example, women often specialise in particular crops and livestock for subsistence and for sale that differ from men's crops and livestock. Women may farm on their own fields, to which they have use rights, and exchange labour with male household members on a formal basis. Even when they sell produce, women are more likely to sell small amounts through local retail markets while men often market larger volumes through wholesale markets or middlemen. Women are more likely to carry their produce directly to market in headloads while men often hire transport. In other words, the nature and scope of the farming operations are quite different, with women having on average less access to the production and marketing resources and training they need for higher returns.

Providing for the special needs of independent women farmers in settings such as sub-Saharan Africa thus becomes a high priority for planners concerned with food production and rural employment. Elsewhere, however, the sexual division of labour in agriculture may be very different, with women assisting men in certain operations or else specialising in tasks such as processing paddy or wheat in the household compound. In planning and project design, gender-specific economic analysis of food production and distribution systems can contribute significantly to improving system performance (Cloud, 1984:18). The analysis of women's productive activities within the agricultural system, the identification of factors (such as technology or the returns to labour) influencing women's productivity, and the application of this knowledge to each stage in the project process, are tools that ensure not only gender equity but economic efficiency as well.

(b) The underline urban informal sector /underline of small-scale self-employment -- street vending, for example, or home-based production or services -- attracts large concentrations of women in many areas of the world (Tinker, 1987). The low capital requirements, the ease of entry, and the flexible working hours of many such occupations encourage self-employment but in turn perpetuate overcrowding of some activities and thus low returns. Occupational segregation is often expressed in the extreme form of specialisations within specialisations. Men from one village in Java sell soup on the streets of Jakarta, for example, while women from the same village (and often from the same household) sell herbal tonics. Typical of such sex segregation, soup-vending requires higher capitalisation and results in higher returns than does the sale of tonics (Hetler, 1986).

The urban informal sector is difficult to define precisely. Thus it is not surprising that women's economic contributions within this sector also remain largely undefined both in terms of their labour force participation and the earnings they generate. A review of the literature by the World Bank found that the urban informal sector constitutes over one-half of all employment in Bombay, Jakarta, Belo Horizonte (Brazil), Lima, and eight Peruvian cities, with high concentrations of women and of younger and less educated workers of both sexes (Mazumdar, 1976). Average earnings of female workers were usually about half that of males and with less variability; in urban Malaysia they were about one-third. It is highly doubtful whether women were spending only one-half or one-third of the time on their economic activities as men did, however. Rather, findings such as this reveal the extent to which women's work -- for various reasons -- elicits lower returns in the informal sector than men's work.

Given the importance of informal sector employment to the economy of urban households in general, and the importance of women's participation in the informal sector in particular, an analysis of the policy implications of these income differentials is a compelling topic for planners. For both urban and rural employment alike, the lower average returns to female self-employment means that they have little or no savings or access to credit for investment in non-labour inputs such as raw materials or labour-saving devices. Thus, low productivity is often perpetuated in a spiral of low incomes, low investments and low returns. A planning strategy for identifying, analysing, and redressing the special difficulties women face in small scale enterprises has been proposed by Dulansey and Austin (1984). Suggestions include assistance in locating small-scale enterprises in strategic places, improving women's access to appropriate technology, raw materials and markets, and securing funding sources and training in financial management and product control.

D. Measuring Women's Contributions to Total Family Incomes

The economic returns to labour reviewed above refer to wages or other earnings in cash or kind. Just as the female share of the wage labour force can be measured, so too (from household surveys) can the female share of total family incomes deriving from wages. And just as the female share of the market-oriented labour force can be measured (wage earners plus the self-employed and unpaid family workers in market-oriented activities), so too can the female share of total family incomes deriving from this source. By placing a value on the production and processing of primary products solely for home consumption, one can move directly into the measurement of the female share of family incomes corresponding to the new standard definition of economic activity. A 1964 household budget survey of Beti farmers in southern Cameroon, for example, concluded that the home-produced portion of food consumption amounted to about 45 per cent of total household income. Given that men contributed a small amount of labour to this task, the conclusion was that about 40 per cent of real family income was provided by women's subsistence work alone (Guyer, 1980:10).

1. Incomes from economic activities as conventionally defined

The methodological complication that intrudes here is how to allocate among own-account and unpaid family workers household income deriving from their joint efforts. Consider, for example, the value of farm production. In this case, the total output of crops and livestock must be measured and priced net of wages paid, non-labour inputs, and losses experienced in transport, storage or marketing (see Connell and Lipton, 1976:53-61).

The simplest way to allocate value among household members is to take the total numbers of hours worked by each member as a proportion of the total hours of family labour and multiply this by the net value of farm production. Each member would thus have "earned" household income in proportion to his or her contribution of time in the group endeavour. In this model everyone's time is assumed to be equally productive and thus of equal value. One could weight the numbers of hours by productivity factors for different age and sex groups, but such weightings are problematic, as we have argued above. (The assumption of equal productivity is also problematic, however, especially for children.) Similar techniques could be used for estimating the value of each person's contribution to other forms of home-based production (e.g., crafts), services, or gathering activities for sale or for household consumption as defined in systems of national accounts.

Table 13 shows the results of a sample survey of individuals from eight villages in Nepal in the mid-1970s in which the contributions to total household income of male and female adults and of children ages 10 to 14 has been estimated. (The value of housework is not included in total income.) The allocation of wage and salary incomes and of pensions to age and sex groups presented no difficulty because the individual contributors could be easily identified. The total value of goods and services produced in other areas (e.g., animal husbandry) was allocated to each age/sex group in proportion to the time contributed by each group to each activity, as suggested above. Both production for sale and for household consumption were included in the income calculations.

When total household income is considered, adult women in this survey contributed almost 50 per cent (column 2) and girls aged 10 to 14 contributed almost 4 per cent (column 4). The great bulk of family income came from agriculture, to which girls and women contributed slightly over half, and secondarily from food processing, to which girls and women contributed almost 90 per cent. Men contributed the lion's share of incomes from wages and salaries and from trading, however, and boys and men contributed slightly over half of the incomes derived from animal husbandry. Note that girls produced more income than boys in all activities, including wage and salary work.

The importance of this analysis for planners lies in the contrasts between wages and salaries, on the one hand, and the wider scope of income-generating and subsistence-oriented production, on the other. If one were to limit oneself to the wage labour force concept, the female contribution to total household incomes is about 22 per cent. But by considering a broader range of market-oriented production plus production for the household's own consumption -- that is, by incorporating the new international standard definition of economic activity -- the female contribution rises to 53 per cent.

Additional analysis would reveal important seasonal fluctuations in women's contributions and variations by location, class, ethnicity, and other household and community characteristics. Several general points deserve emphasis. First, the value of women's economic contributions to the household relative to men's is almost always inversely related to social class. Second, the proportion of households headed by women -- that is, with no male spouse or partner present, or where the male spouse or partner is unemployed or unable to work -- is also inversely related to social class and varies sharply from country to country (Youssef and Hetler, 1983). The assumption that most households contain male workers can be highly misleading. Third, recent research in sub-Saharan Africa, the Carribean, and South and Southeast Asia has identified patterns of

Table 13. Contributions (in rupees) to total household income, and per centage of total contribution of male and female adults and children ages 10 to 14, eight villages in Nepal, mid-1970s

| Activity | Adults 15+ | | Children 10-14 | | Total (5) |
	Male (1)	Female (2)	Male (3)	Female (4)	
Animal husbandry	69,115 (47.0)	50,069 (34.0)	12,440 (8.4)	15,590 (10.6)	147,218 (100.0)
Agriculture	458,271 (45.8)	490,197 (49.0)	18,615 (1.9)	33,728 (3.4)	1,000,811 (100.0)
Hunting and gathering	40,589 (43.7)	45,289 (48.9)	1,793 (1.9)	5,211 (5.6)	92,882 (100.0)
Manufacturing	15,698 (43.0)	19,899 (54.6)	332 (0.9)	536 (1.5)	36,465 (100.0)
Food processing	30,054 (10.8)	236,878 (84.8)	2,544 (0.9)	10,092 (3.6)	279,568 (100.0)
Profit from trading	58,220 (60.3)	38,283 (39.7)	-	-	96,503 (100.0)
Wage and salary	154,902 (77.0)	42,932 (21.3)	1,385 (0.7)	1,925 (1.0)	201,144 (100.0)
Total household income	826,853 (44.6)	923,547 (49.8)	37,109 (2.0)	67,082 (3.6)	1,854,591 (100.0)

Source: Acharya and Bennett, 1982, p. 63.

separate and distinct household income streams and expenditures, where males and females meet financial responsibilities to the family on their own account with little or no access to each other's cash or other resources (Cloud, 1984:25). The assumption that incomes or even knowledge and new technologies are pooled within the household can also be highly misleading, resulting in misguided interventions that lead to unanticipated negative outcomes.

2. The value of housework

We turn finally to the question of what economic value to place on women's, men's, and children's contributions to housework -- that is, to the value of household production and services corresponding to the total labour force concept. As noted earlier, these domestic activities include meal preparation, cleaning the dwelling and surroundings, care of clothing, personal care of dependent household members, shopping related to these tasks, and associated activities such as household repairs, food preservation, and so on. The performance of services that could be done by paid workers (e.g., cooking, child-care) or the production or processing of goods that could be purchased in the market (e.g., sewing clothes) are considered "economic" in this definition although they are excluded from national income accounts (United Nations Department of Economic and Social Affairs, 1968).

Numerous approaches have been used for estimating the economic value of domestic activities. Goldschmidt-Clermont (1982 and 1987a) groups these approaches into four broad categories:

(a) the volume of labour inputs measured by time (e.g., total hours) or number of workers. Based on time-use surveys or censuses, these indicate the consumption of labour resources by domestic activities and labour force activities. They do not provide information on labour productivity, however, and thus on the respective contribution of domestic and labour force activities to national income or household consumption.

(b) the value of labour inputs estimated from the volume of labour inputs together with a variety of wage imputations. For instance, the wages of domestic servants, average wages or wages forgone in the market are applied to unpaid labour time expended in domestic activities. Based on time-use surveys and wage statistics, this method requires information on paid workers able to substitute for the unpaid household worker.

(c) the volume of output measured in various physical units (e.g., number of meals prepared, amount of food processed, number of children cared for, amount of wild food collected, buckets of water carried, or weight of fuel gathered).

(d) the <u>value of output</u> estimated from the volume of output together with price imputations. For instance, value-added in meal preparation can be obtained by using the price of equivalent meals purchased in the market after deducting the value of non-labour inputs (food ingredients, fuel consumption, etc.). This approach assesses the "expenditure-saving" aspect of domestic activities, i.e., the value of the forgone expense resulting from household production. Based on household surveys and price statistics, this method depends on information on the availability of market goods and services of equivalent quality. When the market does not offer equivalent products, alternative approaches to value-added or returns to labour in other subsistence activities can be used (Goldschmidt-Clermont, 1987b:13-16).

The choice of one approach rather than another depends on the uses for which the data are wanted. For most purposes, a combination of methods is needed. For instance, in order to monitor economic development it is necessary to combine volume of labour inputs (time-use data in the first method) with value of output (value-added in the second method).

As noted earlier, available estimates for developing countries suggest that domestic activities account for approximately 40 to 45 per cent of total labour time of all household members and the value of domestic work (as variously assessed) may account for 25 to 50 per cent of measured gross national product (Goldschmidt-Clermont, 1987a:58-9). One interesting example is a 1976-77 survey of urban and rural households in Peninsular Malaysia in which the inclusion of housework raised the estimated total average household income by approximately one-third (only the contributions of persons aged 15 or more were counted). In this survey, 64 per cent of estimated total household income came from wage and business income and from capital and interest (called "market income"); an additional 11 per cent came from transfers, the value of housing services, income from cottage industry and in kind (resulting in "total observable income"); and an additional 25 per cent came from the value of domestic activities (resulting in "total actual income") (Kuznic and Da Vanzo, 1980). The female <u>share</u> of total actual income would also expand signficantly as one moves from wage income to market income to observable total imputed income.

Estimates of the economic value of domestic activities are not simply an academic exercise of interest only to researchers. They are of major interest to planners involved in monitoring economic activities, national economic growth, and the utilisation of human resources (Goldschmidt-Clermont, 1987a:55-62). It makes sense to include all aspects of production for the household's own consumption including the significant economic contribution of domestic work. Only in this way can the true quantity of economic activities, and the true relationship between market and household production, including the transfers between them, be adequately understood. And only in this way is the actual contribution of women to household and national economies fully revealed.

V. CONCLUSIONS AND POLICY IMPLICATIONS

Women's economic contributions to development are multi-dimensional in nature. Several key dimensions have been examined in this paper: (1) <u>labour force participation</u> in different sectors of the economy, as revealed in economic activity rates and the distribution of workers by occupation and employment status; (2) <u>time use</u>, as measured by hours spent in a variety of economically productive activities; (3) <u>labour productivity</u>, as defined by the volume of output per unit of time invested; (4) <u>returns to labour</u>, including both economic and social aspects and both paid and unpaid labour; and (5) <u>contributions to household income</u> according to different criteria of what constitutes "economic" activity. Other dimensions of economic activity could be added. Questions of unemployment and underemployment, for example, are highly relevant to our understanding of women's economic contributions but have not been included in this analysis.

Within each of the five dimensions of economic contributions defined above, we have attempted to review briefly some of the methodological problems in defining and measuring economic levels and trends. We argue throughout that the contributions of girls and women to household and national economies are more vulnerable to measurement error than are those of boys and men. Thus, the validity and reliability of aggregate national indicators of labour force participation, for example, or of measures of individual or household incomes, depend to an exceptional extent on how the female component has been measured. Planners must be aware of the gender bias inherent in many of the conventional measures of economic behaviour. The pervasive underreporting of women's contributions can lead to highly misleading conclusions about economic levels and trends, resulting in inappropriate policies and programmes.

Three major recommendations emerge from this review.

First, <u>economic indicators and other statistical data relating to population, development, and human resource planning need to be scrutinised closely in each country for possible gender bias resulting from the ways in which economic and labour force concepts are defined and the ways in which these data are collected.</u>

We have stressed in this paper problems in the measurement of labour force participation, pointing to examples of extreme bias in some current practices and proposing several possibilities for improvement. But the review identifies similar problems in the measurement of labour productivity, returns to labour (especially in subsistence agriculture and the urban informal sector), and the value of household work, that also conceal large portions of women's contributions in official statistics. A revised system of data collection would not only measure women's contributions (and thus total economic activity) more accurately; it would also facilitate the analysis of sex differentials in each sphere of activity with the purpose of identifying problem areas and designing appropriate development policies and programmes.

When disaggregated by sex, economic analysis can provide convincing efficiency arguments for removing institutional barriers to women's productivity. But it is necessary to begin with good data that includes a specification of the productive activities in which women engage and the resource base that women command (Cloud, 1985:46). In the agricultural sector, for example, measures of the productive activities of household members, specified for planning purposes by age and sex, could include: (1) the amount of labour time and percentage of total household labour time each person spends on crop and livestock production (according to type of crop, type of livestock, location of the work), on production within the household, on informal market activities, and on wage labour; (2) the access of each person to land, capital, markets, agricultural and household technologies, education and training; and (3) the decision-making authority of each person with regard to labour and non-labour inputs, the management of the labour process, the distribution of goods and services, and control over the income or other returns to labour (Cloud 1985). By constructing an "activity profile" of agricultural households, the full extent of each member's contributions is measured and institutional barriers to improved productivity and earnings can be identified and addressed for women, men and children.

Second, improved indicators reflecting the full extent of women's economic contributions and the gaps between women and men in their access to important economic resources are necessary for successful development planning. These indicators can be used for a number of purposes, such as the following:

(a) Monitoring the impact of macro-level economic, demographic and social change on the well-being of women, men, and families. Examples of macro-level changes with potentially discriminatory outcomes are shifts in the international division of labour (e.g., the rise or decline in each country of export-oriented enterprises of various types or of foreign labour markets); the imposition of national austerity measures (e.g., wage freezes, the cessation of some food subsidies, shortages of imported intermediate products); or intensified population pressures on the land, schooling, employment, health services and other institutions. Each of these processes can result in the selective displacement of women from the labour force, for example, or their further marginalisation within the labour force into positions of low productivity and returns, or intensified discrimination against girls and women in access to schooling, health care and other resources. The differential impact of change on women and men should be analysed in the

68

context of geographic location, ethnicity, caste, class, age, and household size and structure, among other relevant characteristics.

(b) Identifying problem areas and planning needs. These include pinpointing significant gaps between women and men in access to productive resources and employment opportunities in different sectors of the economy. Programmes and policies to overcome these inequities include (but are not limited to) the elimination of discrimination against girls and women in all aspects of education and training; special vocational training for women in occupations where they are currently excluded or greatly underrepresented and where there is a demand for labour; wage and salary policies that eliminate discrimination based on gender; technical assistance and extension services to self-employed women (as well as men) in agriculture and in the urban informal sector; credit programmes and policies that actively solicit women borrowers and understand their special needs and difficulties; the legal protection of women's property rights; and research at the national and local levels on existing constraints to the full utilisation of female resources and on the steps needed to overcome them.

(c) Assessing the impact of development projects on women. At the local and district levels, indicators such as those reviewed in this paper collected from sample surveys are vital to the identification and design of specialised or integrated development projects of various types, to project monitoring, and to the evaluation of the distribution of project costs and benefits (Dixon, 1980). Without appropriate data on the sexual division of labour, projects may be mis-directed and ineffective. For example, training programs in animal husbandry or poultry raising are often aimed at men when it is women who do most of the actual work involved.

Much of the literature on the role of women in economic development has stressed the negative impact of many projects on women when measured either in absolute terms or relative to the impact on men (e.g., when men capture most of the economic benefits but women are required to invest additional labour, or when employment opportunities in new industries go to men while competing traditional activities done by women are lost). The cumulative lessons from past successes and failures could provide an important guide for planning future projects. In addition, data on the sexual division of labour in particular productive activities in a project area can be applied to a simulation model to predict potential negative impacts of project interventions on women and try to avoid them. An excellent example of this type of analysis has been done for an agricultural project involving a package of new technologies for small farmers in Nigeria (Burfisher and Horenstein, 1985).

(d) Stressing the linkage between women's productive and reproductive roles. There is a strong linkage between women's reproductive and household roles and their productive roles. A major part of gender inequalities in the labour market, in wages and incomes and in activity patterns can be traced to societal stereotyping of men and women that are related to women's reproductive roles, and to women's responsibility for child-care and housework. In turn, high fertility and mortality rates in some countries can be traced in part to women's low economic status. These linkages strongly imply that governments interested in improving the status of women, in promoting economic development and in meeting their population's basic human needs should commit themselves to providing safe and easily available family planning methods in addition to facilitating female employment through the provision of child-care and maternity benefits. The double burden of production and reproduction falls especially heavily on women in low income households who are least likely to have access to safe and effective birth control services and whose economic contributions are most crucial for the welfare of the family, especially the children.

(e) <u>Incorporating the issue of gender equity routinely into long-term national planning</u>. As noted in an earlier section, "the woman question" has often been shunted to the periphery of development planning. Rather than integrating women fully into the planning process of every government ministry (e.g., agriculture, industry) and into the heart of national development plans, the tendency in many countries has been to consider women's issues as more appropriate to social welfare ministries or to other agencies dealing with women, children, and the aged. The implication in this approach is that women are "dependents" in need of special protection rather than active agents in the development process.

With appropriate analytical tools and statistical indicators, however, every office engaged in long-term economic planning will come to realise that women are active participants in development and so will realise the importance of incorporating women into all phases of the development process as participants as well as beneficiaries. The creation of monitoring units in planning institutions such as government ministries, research organisations, and international development agencies, combined with a policy of active recruitment of women in planning positions, would contribute to the design and implementation of successful growth strategies of benefit to women as well as men. In addition, a full understanding of women's needs and concerns could alter the direction of development planning itself, emphasing different development priorities

Third, <u>anti-poverty strategies can be successful, in our view, only if they effectively promote female employment, incomes, and training</u>. Women's issues are not separate from development policy issues but are central to them (Ahmed, 1987; Buvinic, 1983). Therefore, they should be incorporated in all aspects of planning in human resources, population and development and not segregated in women's bureaus or other specialised offices or agencies. There is a strong need to shift from strategies for women with a welfare orientation to strategies with a production orientation. A broad range of institutional and technological interventions is

70

required in order to increase women's productivity in household and market activities, reduce income differentials between men and women, and raise the incomes of the poorest sectors of the population. Conventional antipoverty policies that place no specific emphasis on women will tend to ignore the large subgroup of women among the poor who work in home production and in sex-segregated occupations (Buvinic, 1983:20-21).

This paper has presented only a few of the many possibilities for data collection and analysis that have relevance to national planners in diverse regions of the world. It has emphasised the measurement aspects of assessing women's economic contributions to development as a planning tool for identifying problem areas and formulating effective policies and programmes. The challenge for planners is to adapt such proposals to their own country situations as a means of alleviating poverty and achieving more rapid and equitable economic growth and social development.

APPENDICES

Appendix A. Unpaid family workers as per centage of agricultural and non-agricultural labour force, by sex, selected countries
(numbers in thousands)

Country	Year	Agricultural labour force				Non-agricultural labour force			
		Females (1)	% unpaid family workers (2)	Males (3)	% unpaid family workers (4)	Females (5)	% unpaid family workers (6)	Males (7)	% unpaid family workers (8)
Algeria	1966	23	55.0	1,251	10.6	76	1.7	910	1.3
Egypt	1966	126	31.9	3,677	20.6	289	2.0	3,312	2.0
Ghana	1970	773	32.4	1,050	12.5	688	3.5	705	0.8
Rwanda	1978	1,342	73.9	1,130	38.1	28	18.7	155	1.9
Iran	1966	200	46.7	2,929	14.4	692	14.8	2,766	1.8
India	1971	765a	14.1	3,432b	18.0	4,042	7.1	38,868	3.5
Sri Lanka	80-81	659	27.1	1,609	14.0	5,743	5.8	2,072	2.0
Thailand	1970	6,546	87.4	6,624	42.1	1,264	24.5	2,095	5.5
Korea, Rep. of	1970	2,134	77.0	3,012	22.9	1,429	15.4	3,551	2.6
Dominican Republic	1981	40	5.3	366	4.2	321	3.4	553	1.4
Peru	1972	147	30.2	1,418	8.1	581	2.3	1,438	0.8
Chile	1983	24	23.4	484	14.5	963	17.6	1,696	15.7

Notes:

a Excludes 25.0 million female cultivators and labourers of unknown status.

b Excludes 100.6 million male cultivators and labourers of unknown status.

Source: ILO, **Year Book of Labour Statistics**, 1976, 1985, 1986, Table 2B (Geneva, ILO).

APPENDIX B. A FIELD TEST OF QUESTIONNAIRES AND INTERVIEW METHODS

The importance of testing questionnaires and interview methods in sample surveys was stressed in the discussion of measurement problems in Section III.   In this appendix we briefly describe one such methods test drawn from a sample of households in the state of Uttar Pradesh, India (see Anker, Khan and Gupta, 1987 and 1988 for further details). The survey was conducted jointly by the ILO and the Operations Research Group (ORG) of Baroda, India.

1. The purpose and design of methods tests

Methods tests are designed to compare systematically the results obtained from different approaches to the collection of survey data. They provide statistical evidence on how best to collect data, and consequently help to identify those approaches that will result in the most valid and reliable data and eliminate gender and other biases (e.g., undercounts of women and unpaid family workers and subsistence producers) that have pervaded official labour force statistics so frequently.

With a carefully-planned methods test one can answer questions such as the following:

(a) Will a different wording of the questions on economic activity, or a different sequencing of questions, elicit substantially different outcomes for each category of labour force participation?

(b) Will a simplified keyword questionnaire elicit different results from a longer and more detailed time/activity schedule?

(c) Will a short reference period of one week elicit different results from a long reference period such as one month or a cropping season or a year?

(d) How will adjusting the criteria for minimum hours required for inclusion in the labour force affect participation rates for each category of the labour force?

(e) Does it make a difference whether interviewers are male or female, or whether the respondent answers on his/her own behalf or on the behalf of others?

(f) Will different methods of interviewing such as use of self-recording diary or personal interviewing or use of telephone (where feasible), result in different responses?

(g) Do interviewers who have gone through intensive training sessions and who work under close supervision obtain substantially different results in their surveys than interviewers who have had only brief training and work with little supervision?

(h) Are the economic activity rates for males and females, adults and children affected differentially by variations in approach such as those suggested above? Do the variations make a difference in some communities or geographical areas, or among some ethnic, caste, or class groups, but not in others?

These and other questions can be answered systematically by selecting several key comparisons so that different forms of the questionnaire or different interview methods are assigned randomly to the sample of respondents being surveyed.

2. The design of a methods test in Uttar Pradesh

The India survey, which was intended to measure only _female_ labour force participation, was designed to answer the following questions:

(a) Which type of questionnaire provides more accurate data on female labour force activity: a keyword questionnaire (with six keyword follow up questions) or a simplified time/activity schedule (with time-use collected on each of 13 activities)?

(b) Does the sex of the interviewer affect the reporting of female labour force participation?

(c) Are the responses provided by (usually male) proxy-respondents different from those of women who respond on their own behalf (self-respondents)?

(d) Do response biases by questionnaire type, respondent type or interviewer type differ according to the definition of labour force activity used?

The survey was conducted in three districts in Uttar Pradesh State from which one community development block (each with a population of approximately 100 thousand) was selected. Within each sample block, nine villages were randomly selected after stratifying sample villages into three size categories. Within each sample village, 60 households were randomly selected and labour force information was collected on women from 15 to 59 years of age. In all, members of 1,621 households were interviewed.

The study design specified two types of questionnaire (keyword and time/activity); two types of interviewer (male and female); and two types of respondent (self and proxy). The design resulted in eight "cells" of equal size: (1) keyword questionnaire, male interviewer, self respondent; (2) keyword, male, proxy; (3) keyword, female, self; (4) keyword, female, proxy; (5) time/activity, male, self; (6) time/activity, male, proxy; (7) time/activity, female, self; and (8) time/activity, female, proxy.

Based on these data, four measures of the labour force were calculated for each sample woman, including the paid, market-related, and new standard labour force definitions described in Section III. In this way, reported activity rates resulting from the different approaches built into the methods test could be analysed separately for each labour force measure.

3. Results of the methods test

The results of the survey are summarised only briefly here according to each of the major variables of interest.

(a) Type of questionnaire. The a priori assumption of the researchers was that the longer and more elaborate time/activity schedule would be superior to the briefer keyword questionnaire in eliciting information on women's economic activities. While results indicated that neither questionnaire type was inherently superior (in that similar results were obtained on each completed questionnaire type), it was necessary to ask a sufficient number of keyword questions to get the same results as obtained in response to the activity schedule. The broader the labour force definition, the more keywords were needed to be asked.

To obtain estimates of activity rates in the paid labour force similar to those obtained from the time/activity schedule, for example, three keyword questions were needed: (1) "What was your (her) main activity in the past Rabi season?" (2) "What was your (her) next most important activity in the past Rabi season?" (3) Apart from those activities have you (has she) worked in the past Rabi season for earnings?" (emphasis added). The three keyword questions combined produced an activity rate of 10.0 per cent, compared with 12.7 per cent as calculated from the time/activity schedule (including both part-time and full-time workers). The first keyword question alone elicited only a 3.1 per cent activity rate for the paid labour force, however, and the first and second question together only 7.0 per cent in all. These two questions about main and secondary activities are often the only ones used in a census; as such, they are clearly inadequate even for the paid labour force. The third question was necessary to raise the rate close to that obtained from the time/activity schedule. And a fourth and fifth question were necessary to raise the rates to correspond to the activity schedule for more inclusive labour force measures.

For the market-oriented labour force, the time/activity schedule resulted in an activity rate of 31.8 per cent -- three times that of the paid labour force. The keyword questionnaire resulted in almost the same rate (30.4 per cent) with the addition of a fourth question: (4) "Did you (she) do something else in the past Rabi season for which income was earned, such as helping out on a family farm or in a family business or in some other activity?" (emphasis added). Based on responses to the first three keyword questions only ("main activity", "secondary activity", "work for earnings") the market labour force was reported to be just 6.6, 18.1, and 23.6 per cent, respectively.

For the new standard labour force (which includes activities such as processing primary products and caring for livestock), the time/activity schedule produced a female activity rate of 83.8 per cent -- almost three times that for the market labour force. Similarly, the keyword questionnaire produced an activity rate of 88.0 per cent when a fifth question was added: (5) "Many persons (also) help their families by caring for family livestock, processing food for storage, cooking for hired labourers, sewing clothes for family members, gathering fuel for family use. Did you (she) do any such activity in the past Rabi season?" (emphasis added). The inclusion in this question of specific subsistence activities such as crop and livestock production and processing for the household's own use made an enormous difference to the resulting activity rates of these rural women.

(b) Type of respondent. It was anticipated in this cultural setting that proxy-respondents (most of whom were men) would tend to report lower levels of female economic activity than would women responding on their own behalf. However, although there was a consistent tendency for proxy-respondents to report fewer hours of work for women than female self-respondents, there were virtually no statistically significant differences observed between the two respondent types in the reporting of labour force activity.

(c) Type of interviewer. Once again, the researchers anticipated that, due to gender biases, female interviewers would be more effective in eliciting information on female economic activity than would male interviewers. Surprisingly, the seven female interviewers elicited significantly lower activity rates on some labour force measures and questionnaires and significantly higher activity rates on others when compared with the seven male interviewers. The differences were slight in magnitude, however.

(d) <u>Other factors</u>. The researchers also tested the effect on the reporting of female labour force activity of a number of other factors not built into the experimental design of the methods test: (1) presence during the interview of persons other than the interviewer and respondent; (2) accuracy of responses according to the opinion of the interviewer; (3) relationship between the proxy-respondent and the women on whom labour force data were collected. These effects were tested using multivariate statistical techniques that took into consideration the effects of questionnaire type, interviewer type and respondent type. In general, neither the presence of other persons (characteristic of 97 per cent of the interviews) nor the presence of particular types of persons (e.g., spouse) had any effect on the reporting of female labour force activity. Interviews with respondents who (according to interviewers) had difficulty understanding the questions resulted in significantly higher reported activity rates, however, presumably because they received considerable explanation of what was to be included.

3. Implications of the methods test

Results from the Indian methods test demonstrate that rural Indian women have very high economic activity rates and that it is possible to measure their contributions reasonably well on surveys and censuses. To do so, however, survey and census organisations must be very clear about how they define labour force participation and should report activity rates for several different definitions. Also, survey and census questions must be clear and must specifically mention examples of economic activities in the locality regardless of whether keyworded questions or activity schedules are used.

Results also indicate that women tend to engage in multiple labour force activities, each often for relatively little time. This fact implies that it is important to collect information on the performance of many different activities. Otherwise, based on the performance of only one "major" activity, the labour force participation of women will be greatly understated.

In the Indian study, male respondents and interviewers did not cause women's labour force activities to be underreported. For this sample and study area, field work techniques relying heavily on male interviewers and (usually male) proxy-respondents were adequate. The same may not be true in other parts of India, however, or in other parts of the world. Indeed, evidence from a similar methods test in Egypt indicates that female self-respondents reported significantly greater labour force activity (particularly in the paid labour force) than did proxy-respondents (Anker and Anker, forthcoming). Field testing and methods tests of different types of questionnaires and data collection techniques are important for obtaining valid results in diverse social settings.

APPENDIX C. SAMPLE QUESTIONNAIRE ON ECONOMIC ACTIVITY

Two basic approaches are possible when constructing a questionnaire on labour force activity. These basic approaches parallel the two questionnaire types used in the methods test described in Appendix B: the keyword approach and the activity approach. Either, or the two in combination, can be effective in eliciting reasonably accurate information on female labour force activity.

Regardless of the type of questionnaire used, certain common elements are required. First, sufficient information needs to be collected to allow the survey or census organisation to measure different types of labour force activity. This implies that detailed information must be collected (i.e., followup questions asked on each labour force activity performed). If -- as we have recommended in this paper -- several labour force definitions are to be measured and reported, additional information on employment status and sales of products must be collected for each labour force activity performed.

Second, information should be collected on all of the multiple labour force activities in which a person engages. Multiple activities are common to both women and men in the Third World. The implication of this point is that the interviewer should not "stop" asking questions as soon as a positive response to one labour force activity has been obtained but rather, continue with the interview until a complete picture emerges.

Third, it is important to collect information on time-use for each activity performed since many women engage in several labour force activities, each for a relatively small amount of time. Thus, if one were to classify women as not in the labour force if they worked for less than a certain number of hours in the reference period (as is commonly done), then it is critical to add up the time spent in each activity performed.

Fourth, we suggest that information should be collected for two reference periods: for the past week, to measure the current labour force, and for the past season or year to measure the usual labour force. Each concept is important.

Questions on economic activity typically begin with a filter question whose main aim is to divide persons into two categories: those who are employed in the labour force and those who are not (i.e., both unemployed and inactive). This questionnaire is designed to elicit information on labour force participation according to the four definitions proposed in Sections III.B. and III.C. No consideration is given here to unemployment or its measurement.

The questionnaire begins with a specific reference to activities that generated some income during the reference period for the worker or his/her family:

Q1. **Did you perform any activity (Or: Did you do any work) in the past season (Or: year) which resulted in income for you or your family?**

1a. **What type of work was that?** (occupation) [Interviewer: Indicate all of the activities mentioned and fill in 1b-1f for each activity performed]

_____

_____

_____

The keywords and phrases in this question are "work" and "income for you or your family". Question Q1 thus has a monetised orientation and should help identify most of those persons engaged in wage employment as well as many of those persons engaged in business and trading activities that involve sales of goods or services.

It is common for questionnaires to use the keyword "work" and not to use qualifying keywords such as "for income" or "for pay or profit". This is because it is generally believed that they keyword "work" is sufficiently clear. In our experience, however, the keyword "work" is ambiguous and needs to be clarified with an additional keyword or phrase indicating what kind of "work" the interviewer is interested in. Unless this clarification is made in the question itself, the connotation of the word "work" is likely to be oriented mainly toward wage and salary employment. Note that the above question asks whether income was earned for "you or your family". It is important to specify in the question that work resulting in family income is also relevant; otherwise, relevant activities where women are working as unpaid family workers would often be missed.

It is preferable to use a long reference period such as past season or past year, since many persons earn income irregularly or are temporarily absent from work for reasons such as illness or child-care. Examples include working as an agricultural labourer or on a family farm or preparing meals for hired hands only in periods of peak labour demand, or doing petty trading or sewing on an irregular basis. Use of a long reference period makes it possible to identify the "usual labour force". To identify labour force participants in the "current labour force", respondents also need to be asked about whether or not relevant activities were performed in a short reference period. One week is almost always used for this purpose.

Follow-up questions to Q1 for each activity mentioned are indicated below.

1b. Did you do this work for someone else, or was this done for your own business or family enterprise or family farm? (employment status)

- ❑ For someone else [Go to 1d]
- ❑ Own business/family enterprise/family farm [Go to 1c]

1c. (If relevant) **Were any of the products produced sold by you or by anyone else?**

- ❑ Yes, products sold
- ❑ No, products not sold
- ❑ Inappropriate or not relevant question

1d. How many days in the past seven days did you do this activity?   _____
[Interviewer: if respondent has difficulty in providing answer in number of days, obtain information using one of the following categories:]

- ❑ Every day
- ❑ Almost every day
- ❑ Several days
- ❑ Two days
- ❑ One day
- ❑ Not done in past week

1e. For how many days in the past season [Or: past year] did you do this activity? _____

[Interviewer: if respondent has difficulty in providing answer in number of days, obtain information using one of the following categories:]

- ❑ Every day/almost every day
- ❑ Most days
- ❑ About half of the days

❏ Some of the days

❏ Rarely, occasionally

1f. In days when you did this activity, how much of the day did you normally take to do this activity? _____

[Interviewer: if respondent has difficulty in providing answer, obtain information using one of the following categories:]

❏ Full working day

❏ More than half a working day

❏ About half a working day

❏ Less than half a working day

❏ About one hour

❏ Small amount of time

The next two questions are intended to identify those activities that would be excluded from the paid labour force but included in the market-oriented labour force and the new standard labour force.

Q2.   **Even if you did not earn any income yourself, did you do any work such as helping out on a family farm or in a family business, or in some other activity, which resulted in income for the family? For example, did you ... prepare any meals for hired workers? ... help to transport goods to market?...** [list relevant activities]

Q3.   **Many persons (also) help their families in other ways, such as ... caring for family livestock, growing or processing food for the family, weaving cloth for the family, building or repairing the house, fishing, or collecting wild foods, fuel, or fodder...** [list relevant activities] **Did you do any such work (OR: perform any such activities) in the past (reference period)?**

Positive responses are followed by additional questions on the type of activities performed (corresponding to Q1a), whether products were sold (corresponding to Q1c) and the time spent (corresponding to Q1d to f). This will identify persons who should be considered as part-time or full-time workers. The interviewer could also probe with questions similar to Q1b to make sure that none of the activities mentioned in this category earned wage or salary income.

The above questionnaire is designed to avoid the problem of asking respondents first about their "primary occupation" or "main activity", to which women often reply "housewife" even if they do income-generating work. It is also designed to elicit a full range of cumulative, multiple activities for all respondents to reflect the total quantity of economic activities and the relationship between market and domestic work.

An alternative to the above questionnaire would be to use an activity schedule such as that in Figure 4. Interviewers would read out the list of activities and indicate which were performed in the reference period. For each activity performed, additional information such as in Q1a to 1f would be collected.

The main advantage of this schedule format over the question format such as Q1 through Q3 above is its straightforward and unambiguous nature. Its main disadvantage is that it takes longer to complete because respondents must be asked about the performance of each activity listed. A compromise between the two questionnaire formats for those interested in only one or two main labour force activities is to combine the two questionnaire formats. One could begin with a general question (such as Q1) and follow this up with an activity schedule (such as in Figure 4) that is asked only when the general question did not elicit any positive response regarding a labour force activity. In this way, interview time would be minimised and information would be collected on "main" labour force activities.

Figure 4: Activity schedule used in ILO/CAPMAS Methods Test survey for rural Egypt

INSTRUCTION TO INTERVIEWER: READ ENTIRE LIST OF ACTIVITIES TO RESPONDENT, INDICATING IN COLUMN 2 IF ACTIVITY PERFORMED IN PAST 12 MONTHS. THEN FILL IN REMAINING INFORMATION FOR ACTIVITIES PERFORMED

Activity	Did you/she do during past 12 months? mark with ✓ if done	Place of performing activity: inside home/ outside home	Employment status: employee or self-employed/unpaid family worker	For self-employed or unpaid family worker: Amount of family products sold during past three months: nothing, some, half, more than half, all	Amount of time spent in performing activity: Hours/min-utes per day (for normal day)	Number of days in past 7 days	Number of days in past 3 months	Nature of ac-tivity: regular/ seasonal
Farming for family (ploughing, irrigation, gathering, etc.)		outside	self-employed					
Farming for others (ploughing, irrigation gathering, etc.)		outside	employee	NR				
Animal husbandry, milking, making milk products								
Poultry caring and products								
Sewing clothes, knitting								
Making baskets, rugs, bricks, etc.								
Construction, building		inside						
Other industry								
Vegetable or fruit trade				all				
Grocery or petty trade				all				
Other commerce				all				
Service (educational, social, personal, health)		outside	employee	NR				
Government services, other services		outside	employee	NR				
Professional (lawyer, doctor, etc.)			employee	NR				
Any other job			employee					
Any other activity for earning money		outside	self-employed	none				
Gathering fuel			self-employed	none				
Making cow dung cakes		inside	self-employed	none				
Processing food for preservation		outside	self-employed	none				
Fetching water		inside	self-employed					
Processing or grinding grain								
Other activity								

INSTRUCTION: If respondent has difficulty with time concept and giving answers for hours and days, please use the following categories: Hours per day: small amount, about one hour, less than half day, about half day, more than half day, full day. Days in past three months: rarely, some, about half, most, all/almost all.

NR means that this information is not relevant for this activity.

86

REFERENCES

Acharya, M., and L. Bennett. 1982. **Women and the subsistence sector: economic participation and household decisionmaking in Nepal.** World Bank Staff Working Paper No. 526. Washington DC, World Bank.

Ahmed, I. 1987. "Technology, production linkages and women's employment in South Asia", in **International Labour Review**, January-February.

Anker, R. 1983. "Female labour force participation in developing countries: a critique of current definitions and data collection methods", in **International Labour Review**, November-December.

_____, and M. Anker. Forthcoming. **Improving the measurement of women's participation in the Egyptian labour force: results of a methodological household survey.** Population and Labour Policies Working Paper. Geneva, ILO.

_____, M. Buvinic and N. Youssef (eds.). 1982. **Women's roles and population trends in the Third World.** London, Croom Helm.

_____, and C. Hein. 1986. "Sex inequalities in Third World employment: statistical evidence", in R. Anker and C. Hein (eds.). **Sex inequalities in urban employment in the Third World.** London, Macmillan.

_____, M. E. Khan and R. B. Gupta. 1987. "Biases in measuring the labour force: results of a methods test survey in Uttar Pradesh, India", in **International Labour Review**, March-April.

_____, M. E. Khan and R. B. Gupta. 1988. **Women's participation in the labour force: a methods test in India for improving its measurement.** Women, Work and Development, No. 16. Geneva, ILO.

_____, and J. C. Knowles. 1978. "A micro-analysis of female labour force participation in Africa, in G. Standing and G. Sheehan (eds.). **Labour force participation in low-income countries.** Geneva, ILO.

Benería, L. 1982. "Accounting for women's work", in L. Benería (ed.). **Women and development: the sexual division of labour in rural societies.** New York, Praeger.

Blacker, J. G. C. 1978. "A critique of international definitions of economic activity", in **Population Bulletin of Economic Commission for West Asia**, No. 14.

Blades, D. W. 1975. **Non-monetary (subsistence) activities in the national accounts of developing countries.** Paris, Development Centre of the Organisation for Economic Co-operation and Development.

Boserup, E. 1970. **Woman's role in economic development.** New York, St. Martin's Press.

_____. 1975. "Employment of women in developing countries", in L. Tabah (ed.). **Population growth and economic development in the Third World.** Vol. I. Dolhain, Ordina, for International Union for the Scientific Study of Population.

Burfisher, M. E., and N. R. Horenstein. 1985. **Sex roles in the Nigerian Tiv farm household.** Women's Roles and Gender Differences in Development: Cases for Planners. West Hartford, Kumarian Press.

Buvinic, M. 1983. "Women's issues in Third World poverty: a policy analysis", in M. Buvinic, M. A. Lycette and W. P. McGreevey (eds.). **Women and poverty in the Third World.** Baltimore, Johns Hopkins University Press.

Casely, D. J., and D. A. Lury. 1980. **Data collection in developing countries.** New York, Oxford University Press.

Cloud, K. 1984. "Women's productivity in agricultural systems: considerations for project design", in C. Overholt, M. B. Anderson, K. Cloud and J. E. Austin (eds.). **Gender roles in development projects: a case book.** West Hartford, Kumarian Press.

Connell, J., and M. Lipton. 1977. **Assessing village labour situations in developing countries.** Delhi, Oxford University Press.

Dixon, R. 1980. **Assessing the impact of development projects on women.** AID Program Evaluation Discussion Paper, No. 8. Washington, D.C., U.S. Agency for International Development.

_____. 1982. "Women in agriculture: counting the labour force in developing countries", in **Population and Development Review**, September.

Dixon-Mueller, R. 1985. **Women's work in Third World agriculture: concepts and indicators.** Women, Work and Development, No. 9. Geneva, ILO.

Dulansey, M., and J. E. Ausin. 1984. "Small scale enterprise and women", in C. Overholt, M. B. Anderson, K. Cloud and J. E. Austin (eds.). **Gender roles in development projects: a case book.** West Hartford, Kumarian Press.

Durand, J. 1975. **The labour force in economic development: a comparison of international census data, 1946-1966.** Princeton, Princeton University Press.

Farooq, G. M. 1985. **Population and employment in developing countries.** Background Papers for Training in Population, Human Resources and Development Planning, No. 1. Geneva, ILO.

Garrett, P. M. 1976. **Some structural constraints on the agricultural activities of women: the Chilean hacienda.** Research Paper No. 70. Madison, Land Tenure Center, University of Wisconsin, Madison.

Guyer, J. I. 1980. **Household budgets and women's incomes.** Working Paper No. 28. Boston, African Studies Center, Boston University.

Goldschmidt-Clermont, L. 1982. **Unpaid work in the household: a review of economic evaluation methods.** Women, Work and Development, No. 1. Geneva, ILO.

_____. 1987a. **Economic evaluations of unpaid household work: Africa, Asia, Latin America and Oceania.** Women, Work and Development, No. 14. Geneva, ILO.

_____. 1987b. "Non market household production in developing countries". Paper presented at Twentieth General Conference of the International Association for Research in Income and Wealth, Roccadi Pope, Italy, mimeo.

Hart, G. P. 1980. "Patterns of household labour allocation in a Javanese village", in H. P. Binswanger et al (eds.). **Rural household studies in Asia.** Singapore, Singapore University Press.

Hetler, C. B. 1986. **Female-headed households in a circular migration village in Central Java, Indonesia.** Unpublished Ph.D. dissertation. Canberra, Department of Demography, The Australian National University.

House, W. J. 1986. "The status and pay of women in the Cyprus labour market," in R. Anker and C. Hein (eds.). **Sex inequalities in urban employment in the Third World.** London, Macmillan.

International Labour Office. 1976. **International recommendations on labour statistics.** Geneva, ILO.

_____. 1977. **Labour force estimates and projections, 1950-2000.** (2nd ed.). Geneva, ILO.

_____. September 1983. **Recent changes in the international standards for statistics of the economically active population.** Paper prepared for presentation at the Working Party on Employment and Unemployment Statistics, Organisation for Economic Co-operation and Development, Paris, 24-25 October 1983. Geneva, Bureau of Statistics, ILO.

_____. 1986. **Economically active population, estimates and projections, 1950-2025.** (3rd ed.). Geneva, ILO.

_____. Various years. **Year book of labour statistics.** Geneva, ILO.

_____, and Research and Training Institute for the Advancement of Women (INSTRAW). June 1985. **Women in economic activity: a global statistical survey (1950-2000).** Statistical Publication No. 1. Santo Domingo, INSTRAW.

International Research and Training Institute for the Advancement of Women (INSTRAW). June 1985. **The importance of research and training to the integration of women in development.** Research Study No. 2. Santo Domingo, INSTRAW.

_____, and United Nations Statistical Office. June 1986. **Improving statistics and indicators on women using household surveys.** Draft Working Paper. New York, UN.

Kent, M. M., and C. Haub. 1985. **1985 world population data sheet.** Washington, D.C., Population Reference Bureau.

Kossoudji, S., and E. Mueller. March 1981. **The economic and demographic status of female-headed households in rural Botswana.** Research Report No. 81-10. Ann Arbor, Population Studies Center, University of Michigan.

Kusnic, M., and J. Da Vanzo. June 1980. **Income inequality and the definition of income: the case of Malaysia.** Santa Monica, The Rand Corporation.

Mazumdar, D. 1976. "The urban informal sector", in **World Development**, August.

Moock, P. 1976. "The efficiency of women as farm managers: Kenya", in **American Journal of Agricultural Economics**, No. 5.

Mueller, E. 1983. "Measuring women's poverty in developing countries", in M. Buvinic, M. A. Lycette and W. P. McGreevey (eds.). **Women and poverty in the Third World.** Baltimore, Johns Hopkins University Press.

Nag, M., B. N. F. White, and R. C. Peet. 1980. "An anthropological approach to the study of the economic value of children in Java and Nepal", in H. P. Binswanger et al (eds.). **Rural household studies in Asia.** Singapore, Singapore University Press.

Palmer, I. 1985a. **The impact of agrarian reform on women.** Women's Roles and Gender Differences in Development: Cases for Planners. West Hartford, Kumarian Press.

_____. 1985b. **The impact of male out-migration on women in farming.** Women's Roles and Gender Differences in Development: Cases for Planners. West Hartford, Kumarian Press.

Recchini de lattes, Z., and C. Wainerman. 1982. **Female workers undercounted: the case of Latin American and Caribbean censuses.** Working Paper No. 12. Mexico, The Population Council, Latin American and Caribbean Regional Office.

Reid, M. 1934. **Economics of household production.** New York, Wiley.

Sehgal, J. 1986. **An introduction to techniques of population and labour force projections.** Background papers for Training in Population, Human Resources and Developing Planning, No. 4. Geneva, ILO.

Sinha, J. N. 1982. "1982 census economic data: a note", in **Economic and Political Weekly** (Bombay), 6 Feb.

Standing, G. 1977. **Studies of labour force participation in low-income areas: methodological issues and data requirements.** Geneva, ILO.

_____. 1978. **Labour force participation and development.** Geneva, ILO.

Staudt, K. 1985. **Agricultural policy implementation: a case study from Western Kenya.** Women's Roles and Gender Differences in Development: Cases for Planners. West Hartford, Kumarian Press.

Swetnam, J. J. 1980. "Disguised employment and development policy in peasant economies", in **Human Organization,** Spring.

Tinker, I. 1987. "Street foods: testing assumptions about informal sector activity by women and men", **Current Sociology,** Winter.

United Nations Department of Economic and Social Affairs, Statistical Office. 1968. **A system of national accounts.** Studies in Methods Series F, No. 2, Rev. 3. New York, UN.

United Nations Department of International Economic and Social Affairs, Statistical Office, and International Research and Training Institute for the Advancement of Women (INSTRAW). 1984. **Compiling social indicators on the situation of women.** Studies in Methods, Series F, No. 32. New York, UN.

Uthoff, A., and E. M. Pernia. 1986. **An introduction to human resource planning in developing countries.** Background Papers for Training in Population, Human Resources and Development Planning, No. 2. Geneva, ILO.

Wigna, W., K. Suryanata, and B. White. 1980. **Comparison of the results of time-allocation research, using two different recall periods.** Working Paper No. 7. Bogor, Indonesia, Agro-Economic Survey.

World Bank. July 1980. **Employment and income distribution in Indonesia.** Washington, East Asia and the Pacific Regional Office, World Bank.

Youssef, N. H., and C. B. Hetler. 1983. "Establishing the economic condition of woman-headed households in the Third World: a new approach", in M. Buvinic, M. A. Lycette and W. P. McGreevey (eds.). **Women and poverty in the Third World.** Baltimore, Johns Hopkins University Press.

www.ingramcontent.com/pod-product-compliance
Lightning Source LLC
Chambersburg PA
CBHW081507290326
41931CB00041B/3233